ROBERT SCHULLER,
My Father & My Friend

ROBERT SCHULLER,
My Father & My Friend

by Sheila Schuller Coleman

ideals
PUBLISHING CORPORATION
11315 WATERTOWN PLANK RD.
MILWAUKEE, WISCONSIN 53226

ACKNOWLEDGMENT

*Lyrics to the song "Sometimes" by Felice Mancini. Permission -
Northridge Music, Inc. (Page 190).*

ISBN 0-89542-025-2 395

Published by Ideals Publishing Corporation
11315 Watertown Plank Road
Milwaukee, WI 53226
Published simultaneously in Canada.

To my husband, Jim. Through his eyes, I have come to know, understand, appreciate and love even more fully Robert Schuller—my father, and my friend.

ACKNOWLEDGMENTS

I wish to thank my husband, Jim, who kept me going when I wanted to give up, who encouraged me when I became discouraged, who laughed when he was supposed to, cried when tears were called for, and yet was brave enough to tell me when I was being corny. Without him, I would never have been able to write this book.

And of course, a great big thank you to my wonderful parents who so willingly and lovingly supplied all the material.

Table of Contents

Foreword
by Dr. Robert Schuller

Success in any other area, arena, or activity will never generate as much joy as that which comes with success in marriage and the family.

May that priceless treasure of family love—which is my most prized possession—entice and motivate readers of this true story to create their own colony of caring, for that's what our family is and always has been.

I've always believed that a faith, a philosophy, or a psychological theory that fails in the intimacies of the home deserves to be questioned. And a faith, a philosophy, or a psychological theory that produces a superbly successful family, in spite of immense social pressures, must be taken seriously.

It is true that, other than my wife of thirty years, no human being knows me better or has lived longer in the

curtain-drawn privacies of my home than the author of
this book, my first-born child. No one else has had
greater opportunity to hear or to see demonstrated daily
the faith that has been the cornerstone of our life and
our ministry. And she has genuinely understood,
embraced, and applied our Christian philosophy of
possibility thinking in her life at every age level. I'm
proud of the person she was, and is, and is becoming; I
share her justified pride in her husband and her own
successful marriage.

"The faith works—if you work at it." That's the
theme of this book. In a secular society that cynically
distrusts hope-promising, faith-demanding commitments,
we see an inevitable, consequential epidemic of
loneliness.

So—to the lonely readers who are deprived of
childhood memories of similar scenes of secure family
relationships and, therefore, find the images portrayed in
this book difficult to believe, I can only plead, "Believe
me. It's true! This book is true! It's possible to have a
happy family!" And that's the ultimate achievement! To
God be the glory.

Prologue

I looked feverishly at the clock on my nightstand. Seven-thirty! Oh, no! I was going to be late again!

If I were late for school one more time, I would surely be put on detention. So, I leaped from my bed and tore desperately through my closet looking for something to wear.

Just then I heard Dad call, "Sheila! Come here immediately!"

"I can't, Dad! I'm running late!"

"I said 'Come here,' and I mean now!"

Dad is very imposing and quite frightening when he's upset. His glasses magnify the anger in his eyes. All Dad has to do is look fiercely at me, and I am duly reprimanded.

"What?" I asked him breathlessly.

"I want you to do the dishes for your mother this morning before you go to school."

"Awww, Dad! I can't! I'll never make it in time for school."

"Don't waste time making excuses. Get busy and get them done."

I couldn't believe my ears. There was absolutely no way that I could do those dishes and still be ready for school on time. I desperately resorted to my best defense system against Dad. I began to cry. Boy, did I cry!

But this time, my defense system backfired. Dad didn't sympathize at all. In fact, he got angry, which only made me cry more.

I stormed to my room, tears streaming down my cheeks. I threw my clothes on and hurled dishes from sink to sink.

Dad beeped the horn. Glancing at the clock as I tore out of the house, I saw that school had just begun. I was furious! Of all the rotten luck. I had to be the daughter of such a cruel man as this Robert Schuller!

Dad took me to school every morning. It was part of our father-daughter routine. He would say, "Sheila, listen to this poem." Or, "This Bible verse is fantastic! Repeat after me. . . . " But, usually, he wanted to sing. And he would always have me sing the song with him, repeat the verse after him, or memorize a poem.

This was a very uplifting routine for me until we'd come to an intersection where the car next to us had one of my classmates in it. Dad would inevitably say, "Let's sing it again. This time with *feeling!*" At those times I'd turn my back to the window and pray for a green light.

On this particular morning, however, there were no poems, no verses, and no songs, only deathly stubborn silence. Dad dropped me off, mumbled a good-bye, and left me to face my class. The bell had rung a good five minutes earlier, and my swollen, red eyes told my classmates everything I didn't want them to know. It was a miserable morning!

But along around eleven o'clock, an office assistant brought a note to my teacher.

"Sheila," he called. "Please go to the office."

"What now?" I thought. On the way to the office, I mulled over every possibility as to the summons. "Maybe it's because I've had so many tardies. I'll bet that's it."

But when I walked through the door, I was greeted with the last sight I wanted to see that day—my father.

"Couldn't he let well enough alone?" I thought. "He ruined my morning. Does he have to ruin my afternoon, too?"

He quickly came toward me and said, "Sheila, I've gotten permission to take you out of school for an hour. Let's go."

He led me by the arm down the empty corridor; and after the heavy school doors slammed behind us, he turned to me and said, with tears in his eyes, "Sheila, I'm sorry. I'm so very sorry. It's not that I shouldn't have asked you to help out at home, but I had no right to insist on it this morning without any former warning. I upset you at the time when you most needed my love and support—just before you went to school. And I let

you go without apologizing, without saying 'I love you.'
I was wrong. Please forgive me."

I put my arms around his neck and said, "Oh, Dad,
of course I forgive you!"

Dad continued, "Sheila, I couldn't work until I
knew things were right with you. I asked my secretary to
re-schedule all my appointments, and I got permission to
take you to lunch. Do you want to go?"

"Oh, yes, I'd love to!"

I'm not sure what we were singing on the way to
lunch but it may have been, "Yes, Jesus loves me, my
father shows me so."

Dr. Robert Schuller in a familiar Sunday-morning pose.

1

A Seed Is Sown

The tired old farmer looked over his freshly tilled field. The fragrance of the new soil and the now setting sun brought a warm contentedness to the old man. He suddenly knelt amid the furrows and, lifting his face reverently to the heavens, he prayed, "O Lord, I know my Jennie is past her child-bearing years, but please plant one more seed—in my Jennie. And let it grow and bear a son—a son who will be a minister—who will in turn plant seeds, your seeds of love, in many hearts."

That dear, old farmer was my Grandpa. And the seed God planted in his Jennie was my dad—Robert Schuller. God answered Grandpa's prayer in a far greater way, I'm sure, than he ever dreamed. Although Grandpa's life was in its sunset days, God had planted a seed that was the beginning of a harvest that only He can totally comprehend.

Grandpa never told anyone about that prayer. Even when Grandma became pregnant again, and even when he heard the first cry of his fifth child—a healthy, robust son—even then he kept his prayer a secret. For he never wanted his son to be a minister just because he, Anthony Schuller, wanted it. Rather, he wanted his son to become a minister because God had called him to it.

And God did call. Dad was only five when his Uncle Henry came to visit. He was Grandma's brother and was idolized by all the family. This dashing young missionary, home from his venture to China, created quite a stir when he pulled into the Schuller driveway.

"Oh, Jennie! I've missed you so!" he said as his sister ran to his car and greeted him affectionately. Then he held her at arm's length and looked her over approvingly, "So, you've got yourself another son while I've been gone. Where is he?"

Just then he saw Dad standing at the gate. Young Robert's boyish exuberance shifted to awe as his tall, handsome uncle strode up to him.

"You must be Robert," Uncle Henry said, laughingly, as he ruffled the head of the adoring little boy. And then he added prophetically, "You're going to be a minister someday."

Dad decided right then and there that he wanted to be a minister; and every night he added to his prayers, " . . . Lord, make me a minister when I grow up."

Grandpa and Grandma Schuller with
their granddaughter—me.

It's a good thing that Dad had that calling into the ministry because he surely wasn't suited to farming. Many, many times he was late getting the cows back for their milking at the close of day. He'd spend long hours on the low hill overlooking the meandering Floyd River, preaching enthusiastically to his crazy congregation of cows and corn.

Dad loved to preach, but the "book-learning" was another story. As Dad grew, Grandpa quietly prayed, but Grandma sternly prodded him to do his studying and reading. And no one could ever fool Grandma! She always knew when a person had done the job and when he hadn't.

I know this by firsthand experience. My sophomore year in Hope College, in Holland, Michigan, I went to visit Grandma for my Thanksgiving break.

The first thing she asked me was, "Do you have any studying to do?"

"Yes, Grandma. I have to read two chapters in my biology, and I have to memorize some reactions for chemistry, and. . . ."

"What's chemistry?" she interrupted.

"Well . . . it's the study of molecules, and. . . ."

"What's a molecule?" she interrupted again.

"A molecule? It's a composite of atoms and. . . ."

"Never mind. It doesn't matter if *I* know it. Just *make sure that you do!*"

I couldn't wait to get upstairs and get a little sleep,

for it had been a long, tiring ride from Michigan. "I guess, I'd better get started right away, Grandma," I lied, trying to sneak away for a much needed rest.

No sooner had I hit the bed and found myself drifting off into blissful sleep when I heard Grandma calling up the stairs, "Sheila, Sheee-la! Are you awake?"

"Yes, Grandma, I am." That wasn't a lie. I was awake—then.

"Don't you sleep! It's important for you to get your studying done."

"Okay, I won't sleep."

But I no sooner said that than once again I found myself in dreamland.

"Sheila, Sheee-la! You're not asleep are you?"

That grandma of mine! Did she have a closed-circuit TV in my bedroom? How did she know whether I was sleeping or studying?

I gave up. I went downstairs and walked into the kitchen, where she said, "Now, Sheila, I know you weren't studying. You were sleeping."

I was caught. But later when I complained to Dad about the incident, he only replied, "Oh, Sheila, she knew what you were doing because that was *my* trick."

Dad made it through school, and I passed my tests. Thanks to Grandma!

Grandma's heritage was rooted in Dutch royalty. Her grandfather was a baron, but also a dreamer and a leader. He came to America in 1887 with the dream of starting a Dutch colony in Texas. After being deceived by the oil companies and wiped out by the Galveston Flood, he fled to Orange City, Iowa, a broken man.

Grandma, too, was a leader and a dreamer; but her drives were confined to the farm. Then came her son Robert. He had all the traits of her baron grandfather. He was strong-willed and a man of vision. He could be all their dreams come true.

Grandma pushed Dad when he didn't feel like moving, and she inspired him to keep looking up. She taught him to do his very best and—most of all—never, *never* give up. It was from her drive that Dad learned to be industrious. But the initiative, the adventuresome spirit, the enthusiasm, the zeal, and the stick-to-it-tiveness that he acquired from Grandma were tempered by the gentleness, the thoughtfulness, and the compassion of Grandpa.

Grandpa and Grandma lived in a big, beautiful, old, white house. They moved from their farm when Henry, their first son, was ready to take it over. I spent every summer there with them on that farm and loved every minute of it.

There were five big rooms upstairs, and each had a chest of drawers filled with old memories. I used to drag down armloads of photographs and find myself lost in them as Grandma told me story after story. There was the story of Grandpa's sod house and one about Great-Grandma's cruise to the Netherlands. And there was the tornado story as only Grandma told it:

"Your father had just come home for summer

recess. I was putting a batch of bread into the oven
when Tony (that was what she called Grandpa) came
rushing through the door.

   " 'Hurry Jennie! The sky's getting real black; it
looks like hail. Can you come help me cover my roses?'

   "I had never seen a sky with such pent-up fury. It
was bound to be released at any minute. Then, suddenly,
as the growling swirls took on the shape of a funnel, the
hovering cone dropped from the sky.

   " 'Tony! It's a tornado!'

   "We ran first to the storm cellar, but something inside
me said that we'd never live through it there. We'd be sucked
right into its huge vacuum.

   " 'We've got to get out of here! We've got to go, NOW!'
I pleaded with your grandpa.

   "We quickly got in the car to outrun it. Your dad
watched from the backseat and told us what path it was
taking. It moved so fast, but so did Grandpa. He was
going eighty miles an hour.

   "Finally, your dad said, 'It's gone! We made it!'

   "But we hadn't made it, not *all* the way. We still had
to return home—if it were still there. We drove past one
farm. There were a few branches down, but no real
wreckage. I began to be a little hopeful that our place
would be all right. But then we came to the last hill
before our place. We could always see the tip of our
barn halfway up the hill. We inched our way higher and
higher, praying that the roof of the barn would appear.
My heart began to pound as we reached the hilltop. At
the peak I looked down where the farm should have

been—and there was *nothing*!

"Grandpa turned white. He clenched his fists and he pounded the steering wheel over and over and he cried, 'It's all gone, Jennie! It's all gone!'

"Although it was a terrible blow, I said, 'Tony, it'll be all right. We're strong. We'll build it up again!' And, Sheila, we did. It was very, very hard, but God gave us the strength.

"You just remember this story, Sheila," she said, and she peered at me with dark brown eyes that contrasted with her white hair, pulled back sharply into a bun. "No problem is so big that God won't give you the strength to see you through!"

When I wasn't pestering Grandma with pictures and stories, I'd follow Grandpa to his basement workshop. There he'd tinker with old, broken toys that we had salvaged from the town dump. I loved to watch him work. His snowy hair, softly lit by the low light in the basement room, reflected his gentleness. His love warmed the cool dampness of his hideaway, so there was never a need for the musty corncobs by the rusty incinerator.

Grandpa had rows and rows of cigar boxes filled with nuts and bolts and every kind of fix-it thing. My favorite box was the one filled with dozens of bent-out-of-shape "granny glasses."

While he worked, I would quietly stand and watch him. His gnarled hands, shaky now in his later years, took a toy, taped a little here, put a new wheel on, and dabbed some paint there. And always, before my eyes, a raggedy, old train tooted, a broken dump truck dumped again, rusty gears began to grind, new wheels started to roll, and bright colors spun like a rainbow. Old toys were like new—only better—because they were now "a la Grandpa!" They had been touched by a master, and as they bumped and dumped and whirred, they said to me, "Grandpa loves you."

It is no wonder that Dad emerged from home filled with compassion for a hurting world. He saw before him tired toys being renewed and broken dreams being restored, and, with God's help, dejected lives finding hope. This was the theme of his home, and it was to become the thesis for his ministry.

Dad was twenty-three years old when he was ordained as a minister in the Reformed Church in America. His ordination service took place in his first church in Ivanhoe, Illinois. It was at this momentous ceremony that he first learned the secret of the old farmer.

He didn't know Grandpa was coming. His dad had never left Alton, so he never dreamed Grandpa would brave the trip into the suburbs of Chicago. But then he never dreamed of the secret that Grandpa was about to share, either.

Grandpa took the bumpy bus ride to Chicago and then hailed a taxi to take him to the church. The journey took him longer than he expected; but finally, he stood at the foot of the stairs of the gleaming white church.

The music was floating through the doors, so he knew that the service had already begun. Pausing a moment, Grandpa looked up at the cross resting on the tall, narrow steeple.

"Thank You!" he prayed.

And then my dear, old, bent-backed Grandpa, with the aid of his cane, climbed the stairs and stood at the back of the church. There he watched with tears shimmering in his eyes as his robed son was ordained into the ministry. Dad said, "Yes" to the calling deep within; and God said, "Yes" to a dear, old man of deep, deep faith. That day Grandpa told Dad how he had asked God to send a son, and let that son be a minister.

It wasn't but ten years later that Grandpa again gazed gratefully upon a cross gracing the heavens. By this time, Dad's ministry had moved to California. He had built a church from scratch and was sharing his messages of hope with thousands of people each Sunday. God had blessed Dad's ministry from the moment he was ordained, and Dad never forgot the tremendous sense of destiny he had felt surge within him when Grandpa shared with him his secret.

Now Dad was launching a new ministry, watching a dream come true. He dreamed of a building, a tower that would house offices and Sunday School classes for the growing church. At the top of that building, there would be a chapel where people could look out over the world and sort out their own problems. He envisioned a

"Dad said, 'Yes' to the calling deep within." The seed
sprouts and prepares to bear its first fruit as Dad accepts his
first church assignment: Ivanhoe Reformed Church,
Ivanhoe, Illinois, 1950.

twenty-four hour telephone counseling service where
people who were hurting, desperate, alone, ready to cash-
in, could reach out in hope one more time by dialing the
letters *N-E-W-H-O-P-E* and talking to a counselor who
cared and could, indeed, give them new hope.

To top it all off, Dad dreamed of an illuminated
ninety-foot cross which would be a beacon to all the
world. Many people told him it couldn't be done. The
engineers said, "Bob, there's no way that we can put up a
cross that high without wires or braces. Why, it'll topple
in the first breeze that touches it."

"If they can send a man to the moon," he retorted,
"then certainly there is someone somewhere who can
design a system whereby a cross can stretch into the sky
all on its own."

The day came when they found a way. The cross
was going to be raised. Grandpa took the train from
Iowa and he and I (as I had been excused from school
for such a monumental event) were going together.

It is one of my last memories of him. He stood by
me, this eighty-three-year-old man, and watched as the
giant crane slowly lifted the bottom half of the cross.
Then the top half went up. Then, as the cross stood
there, its arms inviting the world to come to it,
Grandpa's eyes glistened. God had truly answered his
prayer. The Tower of Hope with its illuminated cross
would draw millions to Christ who, like Grandpa and
his toys, would take dejected hearts and broken lives and
make them new again.

Grandpa went home to be with his God less than a

year later. And God only knows how many lives have been spared from suicide and have found new hope through the Tower of Hope. All because a dear old farmer cared and dared to ask God to plant a seed—a seed watered with much prayer and tended with such care, that an earthly father could then rejoice in the first fruits of his harvest.

What a beautiful lesson I learned from Grandpa. It matters not whether we are in the dawning or in the sunset of our lives when we plant the seed; what matters is that we plant it, now! "For only God can count the apples in one seed."

2

"Whither Thou Goest"

The lithe, young country girl slipped onto the organ bench in the empty little church. She dusted off the music holder and sighed to herself, "Finally! I sure do wish I had more time to practice."

Then, as she donned her well-worn organ shoes, she was swept away by her dream. She could see her shoes, not in brown and patched leather, but in red and sparkling patent, dancing across the pedals. Her hand-me-down dress became a beautiful, flowing gown that tumbled over the organ bench from her waist. As her fingers played across the keys and mastered the sounds of the mighty instrument, she could feel the rafters of the old, country church swell to cathedral proportions.

She was so lost in her daydream that she never heard the door open. Nor did she see the handsome

young man who watched her admiringly. "Hello, there,"
he said, finally.

"Oh! You startled me."

"I'm sorry," he quickly replied, "I guess you didn't
hear me come in. You were pretty involved. That must
be why you play so beautifully. Let me introduce myself.
I'm Robert Schuller, the visiting minister here this week.
And you must be Arvella."

"Yes," she answered shyly. "I suppose you want to
discuss the hymns for this Sunday."

That was precisely why he had come in search of the
organist of Newkirk Reformed Church. But to his
surprise he had found not only an organist but a
beautiful young girl, apparently unattached, for her
hand, he saw, had no ring on it. He had difficulty
concentrating on the hymns, especially when he'd look
up to see her gorgeous blue-green eyes peering gently
back at him. He was stunned by their beauty, their
depth, and their sensitivity. Robert Schuller quickly felt
his heart run away with him. He no sooner got home
from their meeting than he decided that this Arvella
DeHaan was the girl for him. In fact, after only one date
he wrote to his best friend at Hope College, "Bill, I've
met the girl I'm going to marry."

And he did. The thing that amazes me is that Mom
and Dad took so long to find each other, especially since
both were raised in Newkirk, Iowa. Newkirk is not the
kind of town a person gets lost in. It consists of a
general store on one corner, a church on the next corner,
the school on the third corner. And the fourth corner is

a great big cornfield.

Newkirk is a farmer's town. Whatever a farmer might need is supplied by the general store, the church, or the school. The main road leading through town is paved, but the other roads are gravel. If a person were to ride through Newkirk today, he would find it much the same as it was when Mom and Dad were growing up there.

Tiny Newkirk High. All 74 students seen here in 1943. Mom and Dad are two of them—so close and yet so far away.

Four years later, Mom graduated from Newkirk, as Dad graduated from Hope.

Just last summer I was there with my husband, Jim. Grandma DeHaan, my mother's mom, took us on a tour of Newkirk. After we saw all the main attractions, we turned down the gravel road to my uncle's house. Grandma's fifty-six Chevy bumped and bounced along at speeds not generally associated with the elderly. The dust rose in billows behind us, and only rows and rows of corn stood before us. Here and there we could see a clump of trees set back from the road and the rooftop of a quaint, old farmhouse and barn.

Neighbors are separated by miles of farmland but connected by party lines and church activities. I guess that is why I am so amazed that Mom and Dad could have been raised in the same community, attended the same school, shared the same party line, and still have taken so long to find each other.

Dad was four years ahead of Mom in school, but he was a good friend of her older brother Johnny. John is a terrific singer, and Dad is a "ham." These two loved to get together and put on talent shows for school that surely should have put Newkirk on the map. Mom says, "Your father was the life of the show. He was an absolute clown who loved to steal the scenes."

Mom watched Dad and knew about him, but she was very much in the background until after he graduated from high school and left for Hope College. Then she became involved in the music department. She sang in a mixed quartet that competed in all of the contests and won every one except all-state competition, the first place award in the whole state of Iowa. Instead, the quartet came in second. Mom claims it was because they didn't obey their teacher. This is her story:

"When we arrived in Iowa City, we checked into our rooms and freshened up. We had to rehearse the rest of the day, but at supper, we thought, 'Now we can have some fun.' Instead, we were given the order, 'Go directly to bed!' Now, we weren't about to go to bed. After we were sure Miss Iles was asleep, we sneaked out to the carnival that was in town. There was this terrific roller coaster, and it was so much fun that we rode it over and over, screaming all the time. Well, you can guess what happened, can't you, Sheila? The next morning we were hoarse and couldn't sing. Of course, Miss Iles found out—after we lost the competition."

While Mom was finishing up high school, Dad was working his way through college. Grandpa and Grandma Schuller didn't have much money, so Dad took odd jobs to meet the tuition requirements. Lest I mislead you into thinking that Dad's college days were hard and grim, I must say this. Dad is a prankster and believes in having a good time. And I understand from his former classmates that life in the dorm was filled with lots of good, clean fun.

When Dad wasn't studying or working or playing a joke on someone, he was singing in a quartet. He and his three buddies toured the country one summer as the "Arcadian Four." They had to raise all their financial support, but the experiences they picked up along the way made every effort worthwhile.

It was during their tour of the West that Dad met and fell in love with California. This farm boy, who'd seen little more than cornfields, was awestruck by the palm trees, the orange trees, and the perennial sunshine. He decided right then and there that he'd be back.

After college came seminary. It's not easy becoming a minister in the Reformed Church in America. Like many denominations, they require four years of college, three years of seminary, and at least one summer on assignment.

One summer Dad received his assignment. It was with an Indian reservation mission in Nebraska. He lived there and became the friend, the chaplain, and the counselor of the Indians. It was here that he probably had the most hair-raising experience of his life.

One night, the teenage Indian boys and girls were gathered around Dad at the fire-ring. His guitar sang out in the night along with the young people. Suddenly, Dad noticed a large shadow at the edge of the group which moved closer to the ring. As it did so, the light from the fire reflected on black skin. This puzzled Dad, for a black man is a rare sight on an Indian reservation. The young people near the edge of the ring motioned to the stranger to join them.

After the vespers ended and all the young people had gone, Dad noticed that the stranger had lingered behind. "Can we help you?" he offered.

"I don't know. I'm just travelin' through 'n' I don't

have no place to spend the night."

"Well, I think we can help you out. There's an extra cot in my basement. It's not much, but you're welcome to it."

"Thanks. Don' mind if I 'cept your offer."

Dad got him settled for the night and fell into bed. He prayed before he drifted off to sleep, as he does every night, for God's guidance and protection.

Just as he felt the peace of nightfall envelop him, the door to his bedroom flew open. There stood his guest, his eyes shooting fire, his nostrils flared. "Get up!" he yelled at Dad.

"S-sure." Dad could see that he was in no position to argue. His heart was pounding furiously, and his mouth went completely dry. "What could he possibly want?" he thought.

The stranger's eyes pierced Dad's. "Follow me!"

Dad could tell by the look in his eyes that this man meant business. There was no telling what he would do if he didn't follow him.

He led Dad down to the cellar where he had obviously been rummaging through the boxes. Then, turning to face Dad, his eyes flaming, he announced, "I am an angel of God. I have been sent to destroy this mission, for I have found *this*!" And he unveiled the source of his wrath—a child's record of *Little Black Sambo*.

Dad gulped. He knew he was in trouble. Then God gave him the idea, *"Play along with him."* He suddenly seized the record from the man as he said with imitated

fervor, "You're right! I am so glad that you have brought
this to my attention. We must destroy this work of the
devil immediately!" And with that, Dad smashed it to
smithereens!

This seemed to appease the stranger, and he calmed
down a little. Then, he turned on his heels and left,
muttering something about "attendin' to my Father's
business." Dad waited until the wild man was out of
sight, then he quickly called the police. He described the
incident and the man, and then he began to tremble as
he heard their report.

"He sounds like a man we've been looking for, Mr.
Schuller. He escaped from the mental institution here in
town this afternoon. Why, we've had search parties all
over looking for him. He's extremely dangerous. I'm
mighty glad that you are all right. Now that we have a
general idea where he is, we should be able to pick him
up right away. Thanks for your help!"

Dad shakily replaced the phone receiver in its cradle
and then dropped to his knees, "*Thank you, Lord!*
Thank you *so* much for guiding me and protecting me. I
love you!"

While Dad was busy preparing himself for the ministry,
Mother was trying to prepare herself for her dream. She
wanted to be a concert organist. She wanted to go to
college and pursue her career, but her plans were
interrupted by World War II. When her two older
brothers, Johnny and Frank, left for the Pacific and

Germany, Mom was needed at home to help out with the family. Somebody had to help Grandpa with the field work and Grandma with the remaining four children. This left little time for her love—the organ. She did her chores as quickly as she could, and then she'd slip away to the church to practice. It was on just such a day that she met Dad. This handsome preacher came along and changed her life altogether. One year later, Mom left home, friends, and her dream for him.

They married; Dad graduated from seminary and was ordained as a minister of the Reformed Church in America—all on the same weekend. Their honeymoon was pretty short and was almost cut shorter when Mom caught more fish than Dad. Then, to make their life even more complicated, I came along after only ten months.

It wasn't long before Dad had built up a reputation in Ivanhoe. People from miles around were talking about this dynamic young minister. Dad, however, has never been one to rest on his successes. He thrives on adventure; so before long, palm trees, orange trees, and sandy beaches beckoned him. They had implanted themselves in Dad when he first saw them on his tour to California. When the denomination asked him to start a new church there, he eagerly agreed.

Mom wasn't quite as eager. Actually, the thought of going to live in this "foreign country" frightened her, but she loved her man and would have followed him to the ends of the earth. So, we became California-bound.

When we arrived, two thousand miles from everyone we knew and loved, we were faced with the reality of the

"Whither thou goest . . ." Mom and Dad become man and wife on June 15, 1950.

"nothingness" of a new church. There was no office, no sanctuary, no members—nothing! There were only the tiny home the denomination had procured for us and the five-hundred-dollar gift from the Ivanhoe Reformed Church.

Dad's first step was to find a place where we could hold worship services. He checked the Seventh Day Adventist Church, since they met on Saturdays. But they said, "Sorry, the Baptists have it."

Then he checked the Elks Club, but they said, "Sorry, the Methodists have it."

One day, after Dad had searched Garden Grove in vain, he came home exhausted. Mom greeted him at the door. "Bob, have you seen this newspaper ad?"

"Which ad?"

"The one about something called a 'drive-in theater'."

This perked his interest. "Drive-in theater?"

"Yes. People drive there in their cars and watch the movies from them. They don't get out of their cars."

"No kidding?" Now, Dad was really intrigued. "May I see that? Hmmm, they're showing *Cinderella* by Walt Disney. Do you want to go?"

Sure she did, and off we went to the movies. It was great fun, and everyone loved the whole idea, especially Mom. She could take my young brother, Bobby, and me in our pajamas. During intermission and a trip to the snack bar, God planted His idea. Dad was waiting for his popcorn and looking at all the people when he felt God ask, "Robert, why not hold church here?"

The idea really hit him. Of course! It would be
great! It posed many challenges, but Mom and Dad
tackled them one by one. First, they bought an organ
with the five hundred dollars they had. Then they
scraped together thirty dollars for a trailer. A real
bargain, you say? Not when you consider that the wheels
were welded to the axle. There was no way they could
change a flat tire if they ever had one! They built a
wooden cross and its braces and, finally, they borrowed
a choir from a neighboring church for the first Sunday.

Then the calls came. They weren't the expected positive
phone calls. Instead, there were many from other
ministers. They just couldn't believe that anyone would
actually hold a church service in that "devil's den."
Although these calls troubled Mom and Dad, they
prayerfully decided to continue with their God-given
dream.

The day arrived. I sat in the front row in Daddy's
car. At first, ours was the only car there, but then others
pulled in.

When it was time for the service to begin, Mom
said, "Sheila, I have to go now. You wait here like a
good girl. I will be up there with Daddy." And she
pointed to him above our car, on the snack-bar roof.

I was so proud of him. He looked so tall and
handsome in his black robe with the cross behind him,
silhouetted against the movie screen.

Then Mom came into the picture as she climbed the

stairs to her perch. She was a beautiful sight. Her feet, though not jeweled and glittery red, still shone as they danced in the California sunshine. Her robe, though not of silk, fell in soft warm folds from her organ bench high above the cars. There were no church rafters above to bounce the music along walls, but there was never-ending blue sky and soft, billowy clouds. And Mom sent her love song up to the heavens where it was caught and sent back again.

There was Mom, courageously playing and supporting her pacesetting husband as he extended his arms to the congregation below and declared, "This is the day which the Lord has made; let us rejoice and be glad in it!"

3

Christmas Capers

I was just three the year that Grandpa and Grandma Schuller came to visit us in Ivanhoe. I was still discovering the joy, the beauty, and the wonder of winter.

One day, early in their visit, Grandpa looked out the window. A fresh layer of snow was spread over everything as far as I could see. Every tree, lawn, and rooftop was blanketed in God's white velvet. I broke Grandpa's reverie with a typical three-year-old intrusion.

"Good morning, Grandpa," I said, as I proceeded to climb up on his lap and plant a wet kiss on his wrinkled, old cheek. "What'cha doing?" I asked.

"I'm looking at the beautiful world God has given us. Sheila, have you ever made a snowman?"

I shook my head. "No."

"Well, today you are going to. Come on." And with that, he bundled me up and we braved the blustery cold, Chicago day.

Grandpa immediately set to work. I just watched. A few times, I patted a little here and a little there the way Grandpa did, but that was about all. When he had finished with the snowman's round body, he added the face, piece by piece. Then, he topped him off with his hat and scarf and said, "There you go, Sheila. Meet Mr. Snowman."

I was very impressed with this darling man of snow. "Oh, Grandpa! I love him!" I cried as I tried to hug my new friend. My little arms couldn't begin to embrace his chilly belly.

We had been outside for over an hour, so Grandpa suggested, "We'd better go in now, Sheila. It's too cold for you to stay outside any longer."

"Oh, Grandpa!" I protested, "I don't want to go in!"

"Come on, Sheila. Really, it's too cold for you out here."

"But I can't leave Mr. Snowman here all alone." I was convinced that Mr. Snowman was a real man with real feelings. "If it's too cold for me, isn't it too cold for him?" And then I had the kind of brainstorm of which only three-year-olds are capable. "We'd better take him inside so he can be warm, too."

"Oh, no, Sheila! Snowmen don't like to be warm. They have to stay really cold in order to live."

"Do you mean that if it gets too warm, he'll die?" I asked wide-eyed.

"Yes, you might say that. Believe me, he can't come in the house. But, look, you can see him from your bedroom window. Let's go inside and talk to him from there."

Well, I must have felt the cold penetrate my coat at that moment, for Grandpa's suggestion suddenly sounded awfully good. So I ran into the house and went straight to my room. I didn't budge from my window all day.

That night I had trouble getting to sleep. "Are you sure that Mr. Snowman will be okay?" I asked Mom as she tucked me under my warm covers. "I hope he doesn't get scared out there all alone in the dark."

"Sssh, Sheila. He'll be just fine. Now go to sleep."

The next morning the sun came streaming through my window. I awoke with a start. "Mr. Snowman!" I ran to the window to see if he were still there.

He was, but he looked different from the way he had the day before. His face was twisted and droopy, not at all like the cheery man I'd said good-night to. By lunchtime I could tell that something was definitely wrong with him.

He was getting smaller and smaller, and thinner and thinner. He was wasting away. "Grandpa! Grandpa! What's wrong with Mr. Snowman?"

"Sheila, I'm afraid it's getting too warm for him. Do you remember that yesterday I told you that snowmen can't get too warm?"

"Y-yes." I really started to get scared. Grandpa had also said that if it got too warm, Mr. Snowman would die!

"It looks as though it's getting too hot for Mr. Snowman. We probably won't get to see much more of him this year. He'll go back into the earth until it gets cold out again.

"Sheila, don't cry. He'll be back next year—and the next. Just as soon as it's cold out again. You'll see."

Poor Grandpa! He didn't mean to make me feel bad. And, he didn't mean to mislead me. How was he to know that we would move to California that year? How was he to know that that snowman was the only one I would ever have?

The year flew by and much happened. Mainly, we moved to sunny California. And here it was Christmastime again. It didn't look like Christmas. It didn't feel like Christmas. But it was.

One day, Dad mysteriously pulled me aside.

"Sheila," he whispered, "how would you like to go shopping with me for Mommy's Christmas present?"

"Okay, Daddy. What are we going to get her?"

"You must keep it a secret. Can you keep a secret?"

"Why? Don't you want Mommy to know what you're getting her?"

"Yes," he explained patiently, "But not until Christmas Day. It's more fun to make it a surprise."

Dad wasn't about to take me shopping with him

until he was sure that I wasn't going to spill the beans. Finally, after lots of answers to my four-year-old questions, he decided to take the risk.

"Come on, let's go. And remember, don't tell Mommy!"

We didn't shop very long before Dad found what he was looking for. The nice lady polished it until it shone, wrapped it up really pretty for us, and then we took it home and proudly put it under the tree.

I could hardly contain myself. I wanted to tell Mom in the worst way what we had bought her. But I didn't dare. Daddy had been very firm about keeping our secret a secret.

Finally, Christmas Day came. Mommy gave me my present, but I wasn't nearly as interested in mine as I was in hers. Bobby opened one of his, doing the best a toddler could, and then Dad opened his. Just as I thought we'd never get to Mom, Dad picked up the present we had bought for her and gingerly handed it to her. "Now, Arvella," he said, "You've got to guess."

"Oh, Bob! I can't," she moaned. "Just let me open it."

"Nope. Not until you guess."

"Well, how about a clue then?"

Dad reluctantly gave in. "A clue. Let's see. . . ."

I was about ready to burst. "I've got one! I've got a clue!"

"What is it, Sheila?" Mom asked.

I took a deep breath and proudly answered, "It toasts!"

Mom looked at Dad, her eyes brimming with laughter. Meanwhile, Dad turned beet-red and groaned.

"Well," she said, "You don't suppose that this is a toaster, do you?"

I couldn't believe it! Mom had guessed! "That's it, Mommy!" I cried, excitedly. I was puzzled as to why Mom and Dad were laughing so hard. I couldn't see anything funny about a toaster.

The next year, it was Mom's turn to pull the wool over Dad's eyes. But where Dad failed, Mom succeeded—a

Just the three of us, 1953.

little too well.

Dad loves to go fishing, and he had been begging for a fishing pole all year long. That had been his favorite pastime on the farm, besides preaching to the cows. In Orange County, though there are few rivers, there is a vast ocean close by with gigantic fish in it.

Dad pestered Mom until he was sure that she had gotten the message—he didn't want *anything* for Christmas except a deep-sea fishing pole. He left notes on her pillow at night and even clipped out ads from the paper.

Finally, Mom got sick of it. "Sheila," she told me, "He's so sure that he's going to get a fishing pole that that's just what he's *not* going to get! It's no fun getting him something when he knows what it is. I want to surprise your father."

She knew better than to let me in on her plan. I had no idea what she was going to do with all those empty paper towel rolls she suddenly started saving. It wasn't until the night before Christmas Eve that Mom let me in on her surprise—and that was only because she needed my help.

"Here, Sheila," she said as she guided me. "Hold these together like this until I get them taped." We taped two rolls together, end to end. Then we added another, and another, and another until we had a tube about six feet long. In the very last one, we tucked a can of shaving cream. We wrapped the whole concoction in Christmas paper and put a big bow on it. Then Mom put the final touch on—a tag which read, "Merry

Christmas to my wonderful husband. With love, from
Arvella."

The next day, she tucked the long, pole-shaped
present way at the back of the tree. It looked as though
someone had tried to conceal it but had failed miserably,
for the ends hopelessly stuck out at both sides of
the tree.

Meanwhile, Dad was very busy at his office, preparing
himself for the Christmas Eve candlelight services. This
was a beautiful tradition that he had started at our
church. Many, many people crowded the little chapel to
sing the carols and hear the Christmas message of hope.
People came hurting and left with new dreams, new
visions. They came empty and left fulfilled. They came
lonely and left with a new love in their lives, Jesus
Christ.

Dad always puts a lot into his messages. He takes
great care in preparing his words and his spirit for every
service. But of all the services, it is the Christmas Eve
service that demands Dad's all, Dad's best.

Dad finally felt that he was ready. He arrived home
fully prepared for the task that lay ahead of him that
night. But as he was walking past the tree, he saw
something that completely wiped all of his hard-earned
preparation from his mind.

"My pole!" he cried. "My pole!" He ran excitedly to
the kitchen where Mom was cooking dinner, and he
smugly teased her, "Arvella, you'll never guess what I
saw under the Christmas tree. It's about six feet long and

it's very, very narrow." Then he added sarcastically, "Now, what in the world can it be?"

Mom couldn't help the little smile that played along her lips. "Why, Bob! I'm not going to tell you what's in there! You'll have to wait until tomorrow to find out."

"Tomorrow!" he cried. "I can't wait until tomorrow! Look! I'm starting a new tradition right now! Every year we get to open one present on Christmas Eve. Then we can open the rest on Christmas Day."

That's when Mom made her mistake. That's when she agreed to Dad's "new tradition." Dad was delighted when Mom said, "Yes, you can open one present." Of course, he ran straight to the pole and opened it with all the eagerness of a child. He merely glanced at the wrapping and the tag, and the paper literally flew from the package. Then he peered down the long tube.

Suddenly, he became very still and very quiet. "Where is it?" he managed to choke out. Then his face brightened, "Oh, Arvella! You tricked me. Of course, you wouldn't wrap it. It's too hard. Where is it? Is it out in the garage?"

Her face was expressionless.

Dad was nearly beside himself. "Under the bed?"

"No, Bob, this is it."

His face fell—hard. He was *so* disappointed. Poor Dad! All the possibility thinking in the world couldn't change that can of shaving cream into a fishing pole.

But possibility thinking isn't the only thing that Dad teaches. He has also said, "It's not what happens to you that matters; it's how you react to what happens to you."

Well, here was one of Dad's hardest tests. Would
he pass?

He looked at the can of shaving cream in his hand,
and then he looked over at my now-penitent mother.

"I'm sorry, Bob. I just couldn't give you a fishing
pole! Not after all the notes you left and 'hints' you
gave. Why, it wouldn't have been a surprise."

"Well, you surprised me all right." Then, he got the
same wicked gleam in his eye I'd seen in Bobby's so
often. "So, it's surprises you want for Christmas, is it?
Well, how do you like this one?"

Before she knew what was happening, Mom had
shaving cream squirted all over her.

"Bob! Stop! Stop!" She screamed as she jumped up
and tried to run away from him.

But Dad was having fun now. He laughed and
chased her from room to room, giving Mom back her
"gift."

Finally, Dad grabbed his soapy, slippery wife and
pulled her close to him.

Sheepishly, Mom looked up through the suds and
said, "I'm sorry. I guess it was kind of a mean thing
to do."

"Yes, it was!" Dad retorted. "But, I love you
anyway. I really do." He tilted her chin so that her eyes
met his. "Merry Christmas, dear," he said with a kiss.
"It's not important that I didn't get a fishing pole for
Christmas, for I have *you*!" After Dad hugged her, he
pulled away suddenly and continued, "But, don't ever do
that to me again!"

An hour later, Dad stood before the congregation and his pretty young wife. The church was gleaming in the light of the candles that lined the little chapel. He looked out over the faces of the many people who had come to celebrate Christmas and the birth of the Christ Child. There were the young businessman and his wife, struggling to keep their marriage together. There was the college girl, wondering if she'd make it through that semester. Finally, there was the new widow. She would be facing her first Christmas morning alone.

Dad took a deep breath and proclaimed, "Joy to the world! The Lord has come! Let earth receive her King!" The choir sang the carols beautifully. The songs swelled within the chapel, and the rafters echoed the good news. Dad's message was as powerful as ever. His closing remarks still ring in my heart. "Two thousand years ago in a dark, candle-lit cave in Bethlehem, a Babe was born. And with Him, Love was born, Hope was born, and Joy was born." Then, he continued, looking at the young college student, "Tonight, won't you weave your dreams around this Babe and find new hope?"

With the young couple in mind, he said, "Tonight, won't you reach out to Him and grasp His scarred little hand and find real, true love?"

For the sorrowing widow, he said, "And, finally, won't you follow His tiny, wounded feet down the pathway to everlasting joy?"

At last his eyes met Mom's. He said, "Truly, *this* is the greatest gift that we have been given—the gift of hope, the gift of love, the gift of joy—the gift of Jesus!"

4

"Preachers' Kids"

Bobby was running around the house pretending to be smoking an imaginary cigarette, when Mom suddenly grabbed him by the arm.

"Young man, if you don't stop that, there won't be any television for a whole week. If that's what it teaches you to do, then you won't watch it! Is that understood?"

At four, Bobby was already a terror. He had these wicked cowboy boots he just loved to swing into my naked shins. And Sunday School teachers were getting scarce. Three had left since they'd had Bobby in their classes.

But this "smoking" pencils and toothpicks was getting out of hand. Finally, Dad pulled him aside and told him, "Bobby, you really shouldn't do that!"

"Why not?"

"Because when you grow up, you will be more likely to really smoke cigarettes."

"What's wrong with that?"

"If you smoke cigarettes, they can give you cancer."

"Cancer? What's that?"

"That is the worst disease you can think of."

This sunk home. Bobby hated to be sick, and the "worst disease" he could think of was bound to be bad.

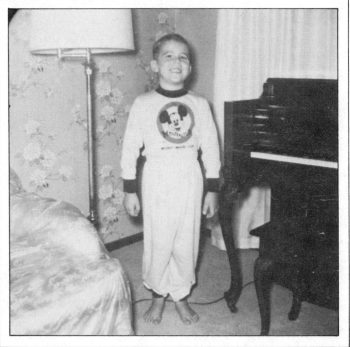

Mischievous Menace—my brother, Bob— the future Rev. Robert A. Schuller.

It worked. And just in time. The president of the Reformed Church, the denomination with which we are affiliated, was coming to visit. It would never do to have Bobby running around "smoking" everything.

Visitors are a common occurrence in a parsonage. Since the home is supplied by the church, it is considered open house for all clergy passing through. Consequently, it was common for someone to drop in unexpectedly and stay for a day, a night, or even a week.

Fortunately, this time we had forewarning of our auspicious guest, this president of our church, Dad's boss. His imminent arrival sent all of us into a flurry as we desperately tried to prepare our humble home for our prestigious visitor.

When he arrived, I could tell that all of Mom's worries were well justified. He was an imposing man, well-bred, reserved, dignified, and proper.

But, all of Mom's preparations paid off. Or so it seemed the first day. But on the second, disaster struck. The request seemed innocent enough. Our guest simply asked Dad, "Bob, would you be free to take me to the Artesia Reformed Church this afternoon?" With Dad's assent he added, "And bring Bobby along. It will be a good experience for him."

They hadn't been in the car very long when our guest pulled out a cigarette and proceeded to smoke.

He then launched into a lengthy theological dissertation, pausing only long enough to take long, thoughtful drafts from his cigarette. Bobby, unable to contain his consternation, suddenly interrupted with, "Ummm! You shouldn't smoke!"

Horrified, Dad desperately tried to hush Bobby up, but the president demanded of Bobby, "Well, for heaven's sake, why not?"

Helplessly, Dad shrunk down into his seat as Bobby pulled himself up proudly and replied, "Because you'll get the worst disease I can think of!"

Totally taken aback, our guest demanded, "And what, pray tell, is that?"

By now Dad was terrified. His thoughts raced to answer the question running through his mind, "What's he going to say *now*?" But Dad could never have guessed what Bobby was about to say.

My little brother, in total command of the situation, looked at our guest squarely and announced, "Diarrhea!"

I'm afraid that my brother and I were the cause for many such embarrassing moments for Dad and Mom. There were certainly many opportunities, for our home was the center of the entire church. In fact, except for the services themselves, which were held in the drive-in, every other activity was held in our home.

Often, when Bobby was chasing me through the house with those notorious boots of his, Mom would stop us with, "Shhh! Daddy's talking to a crying lady. We mustn't make a sound while she's here."

Or we were told, "Please go play outside for awhile.

Daddy's working on his sermon and needs it to be very quiet."

These "quiet times" never bothered me. I understood. I was very proud of the fact that Dad was helping all these people. In fact, I loved to ask my friends what their father did for a living, just so it would give me a chance to brag about mine.

Of all the activities, such as Bible studies and other meetings, all of which were held in our home, my favorite was the choir rehearsals. While Mom and the choir were engrossed in their music, I would sneak into the crowded living room. Tucked away in my hideaway behind the sofa, I would listen to the music for hours. Often I was discovered fast asleep, long after everyone had gone home.

Another of my favorite activities was helping Mom and Dad on Saturdays with the church bulletin. My help on this project, however, was usually limited due to the mess I was prone to make. Every Saturday Mom would pull out the primitive mimeograph machine and the big jar of ink. She and Dad would proceed to run off all the programs, then lay them out on the kitchen table and every inch of counterspace to dry. The only part of the process I was allowed to help with was the folding. I'm sure that there was a great deal of wisdom and experience in that parental decision. You see, they usually managed to get the kitchen pretty well inked without me.

It is no wonder that I grew up with a love for the church and a love for music. I was surrounded with it my entire life! When they were eventually able to build church offices and the chapel, I was busier than ever with church work, for the new site was only a block away from our parsonage.

Those were exciting days! The drive-in had gone over so well that they were able to raise money to build a new church. Daddy was like a kid with a new toy. He was always running over to see how the construction was going. One day he took me along. "Sheila, do you want to come with me to the new church?"

I hadn't seen it yet. I'd only heard about it. "Oh, yes!" I said. So, I slipped my little hand into his big, strong one. I had to run alongside him to keep up with his long strides. We walked briskly down the short, little street, past the other three houses on our block until we came to the corner.

"We're almost there!" he said excitedly. "When we turn the corner you'll be able to see it. It's going to be the most beautiful little church around."

I don't know what I expected, but as a young child I know I expected more than I saw. For when we turned the corner there was—nothing! Nothing, that is, except bare, concrete foundations.

"Isn't it wonderful, Sheila?" Dad was exuberant! He began stepping off the foundations. "Here is where the choir loft will be, and here is where the pulpit will be. I'll stand here and talk to the people over there. You go and stand over there. That's it. Now, let's pretend that it's Sunday!"

I stood where "the congregation" was supposed to be, while Dad stood in the "pulpit." Then he stretched out his arms as he is prone to do and boomed, "This is the day the Lord has made, let us rejoice and be glad in it!"

By this time I was totally captivated by Dad's dream. I felt wonderful and privileged that he was sharing it with me.

"Come on, let's step it off again." His long legs measured off the yards, while my little feet pattered after his.

I was terribly excited about the new chapel. "Maybe we won't have to pull the silly, old trailer to the drive-in anymore!" I thought. And so did Mom and Dad.

But we were all wrong, for we were faced with an unforeseen problem. I learned of it at the breakfast table one morning after a fateful board meeting.

Mom was talking to Dad, "Well, Bob, there's only one solution."

"Solution to what?" I butted in as I stretched my little body halfway across the table, grabbing for the sugar jar.

"Don't interrupt! And don't reach! Ask someone to 'Please pass the sugar.' " Dad always insisted on good manners.

Mother patiently explained, "It's Rosie Gray. Do you remember her?"

I did. "She's the crippled lady who comes to the drive-in, isn't she?"

"Yes," Mom continued. "Someone asked at the meeting last night, 'What will happen to Rosie when we stop holding church services in the drive-in?' "

Dad interjected, "We really must do it! We have no choice!"

"Do what?" I hated being left out—I still do.

Dad continued, "They want us to have one service at the chapel and then go and do another at the drive-in."

And that's exactly what they did do for five-and-one-half years. They went through one total service at the new chapel. Then the organ was pushed into the trailer, and the choir, the Sunday School teachers, the ushers, and Mom and Dad and we kids all packed into our cars and went through the same service at the drive-in.

I loved Sunday School at the drive-in. Since I had been to the service before, I knew all the answers to the questions. And coloring on the picnic tables was always fun, because the wood grain made everything all ripply. But it was especially fun to sneak away and play on the playground equipment. Of course, this was strictly forbidden and was always met with stern punishment.

It is common knowledge, and maybe even fact, that preachers' kids are the biggest brats in the church. Bobby and I were no exception. "My Daddy owns this church, and no one can tell me what to do," was my frequent attitude as I stole sugar cubes from the kitchen and played cowboy on the chairs.

My favorite trick involved Dad. Every minister stands at the back of the church to greet the people after the service. Well, I liked to liven things up. I would dash to the back of the church and stand beside Dad. Everyone who left had to shake my hand as well as Daddy's.

Brats, bums or braves? Certainly not angels!

One Sunday, while Dad's attention was diverted, I managed to slide under his robe. It was dark and warm under there. Then I listened carefully until Dad greeted the next lady. At just the right moment, I stuck out my hand from right about where Dad's stomach was. I chuckled to myself as I thought of my "three-armed Dad."

The lady shook my hand and said with a twinkle in her voice, "Good morning, Sheila."

"Now, how did she know it was me?" I wondered.

Some Sunday afternoons, my organdy dress went up, my ruffly panties came down, and Mom's paddle flattened itself against my bare behind. I have no doubt that I deserved every spanking I ever got.

But Bobby was even worse! And his antics extended into midweek. Then, most of them were directed my way. Finally, I had had enough!

My best friend, Laura, was fed up with her brothers, too. So we decided that the best way to get back at them would be to run away. Then, when Mom and Dad found out that I had run away because Bobby had been so mean to me, he'd get it for sure!

We planned it all very carefully. I pulled an extra pillowcase from out of Mom's linen closet and stuffed it with some clothes, some crackers, and a flashlight. I carefully hid it under my bed (how creative!) and then wrote my going-away note:

Dear Mom and Dad,

Laura and I have run away from home. Please do not worry or feel bad. We did not run away because of you. We left because Bobby and David are soooo mean!

Love,
Sheila

Then I carefully took my note and, when Mom wasn't looking, tucked it between the napkins of the napkin holder. I figured that when they were eating supper that night, they would come across my note, be really mad at Bobby and would give it to him good! My plan was to meet Laura at five o'clock that night. My stomach started to get a little nervous, but I knew that we had to go through with it.

I was just pulling the sack from under my bed when I heard the door open. I must have looked terribly guilty as I turned sharply to see Dad standing there.

"What have you got there, Sheila?"

"Oh, just some dirty clothes." My heart was starting to beat wildly as my mind raced. "What if Daddy discovers my plan?" I thought, but deep down I hoped he would and would talk me out of it.

He peered down at me with his soft brown eyes and gently guided me over toward the bed. "Sheila, sit down here a minute. I want to talk to you."

As I sat next to him, I felt his strong arm as it went around my shoulders. "Sheila, have I ever told you about burglars?" he asked.

"Burglars!" I thought. I'd forgotten about them. But I couldn't let Dad see how anxious I felt about this overlooked consideration. I replied as calmly as I could. "Yes, why do you ask?"

Dad ignored my question and continued, "And have I told you how dangerous it is for little girls to be out-of-doors at night with burglars running around?"

"Yes, Daddy, you have. But why all these questions about burglars?" By now I was nervously tracing the flowered pattern of my bedspread over and over.

"I found your note," he said quietly.

"My note?" I asked innocently, yet inside I was scared. I was sure that Dad was furious with me for wanting to run away. Afraid to face him, I riveted my eyes on the bedspread. Nervously, I asked, "W-what note?" Then I braced myself for the scolding I knew was coming.

But to my surprise his voice was gentle. "Sheila, you weren't really going to run away, were you?"

"Y-yes. Yes, I was! I just can't take one more day of Bobby's teasing!"

"But what about Mommy and me? We would miss you terribly if you were ever to leave us. We love you, Sheila!"

Suddenly, I was overwhelmed by the thought of leaving Mom and Dad. "Oh, Dad!" I cried as I flung my arms around his neck, "I love you, too!" At that moment, with Dad's firm and loving arms around me, the last thing in the world I wanted to do was leave my daddy!

Bobby's teasing didn't get much better, but I was able to handle it now, for I was beginning to see the humor and the love behind it.

Although my first inclination is still to run and get out of a difficult situation anyway I can, I know now that the only real solution is to stop and pray, and to look for the good that can come from it. I learned that day, when Dad held me in his arms, never to run *from* a difficulty, but rather to run *to* my Heavenly Father's arms. When I pray and feel God's love surround me, I know that I can face anything with courage, hope, and confidence!

5

"I Think I Can!"

I took my newly completed picture, folded it carefully, sealed it in an envelope, and addressed it, "Santa Ana Register, Youth Page, Picture Contest." I mailed it proudly, sure that it would be a winner. Ever since I had seen the contest announced in the paper, I had wanted to enter. They announced a new winner every week, and sometimes the winning pictures were absolutely awful. I was positive that I could draw as well as any of them.

The week dragged by slowly. I couldn't wait for Sunday to come so I could see my own picture and name printed as the winner.

So when Sunday finally did come, I jumped out of bed, ran out to the driveway in pajamas and robe, and tore through the paper. But to my utter disappointment, my picture wasn't there. Someone else had won.

Dejectedly, I headed back to the warmth of my home. "How could they have picked that stupid picture instead of mine!" I thought. Just then Dad saw me with the crumpled paper in hand.

"Did you win, Sheila?" he asked anxiously.

My instant flood of tears told him that, indeed, I had not.

"Now, Sheila," he said consolingly, "Sometimes we have to try again and again before we see our dreams come true. You've only entered once and only lost once. I know that if you keep trying, eventually you'll win."

My hopes renewed, I decided that I would enter again. It was almost Thanksgiving, so I decided I'd draw a cornucopia. I was sure that because of the difficulty of drawing the fruit my picture would rate high with the judges.

I carefully arranged the apples, pumpkins, and other fruit, and then shaped and shaded each one until I was sure that it was just right. Again, I sent off the drawing with expectations of winning. And again, I scurried from my room at the break of dawn to get the paper. This time as I opened it to the Youth Page, I was excited by what I saw. There was a beautiful cornucopia! But when I looked closely, I saw it wasn't mine. I had lost again!

This contest wasn't as easy as I had thought. But Dad kept encouraging me. "Keep trying, Sheila. Don't give up!"

"Keep trying?" I thought to myself. "I've already *tried* two times and *lost* two times!" At eleven years of age, I didn't have much patience or persistence.

Christmas, now, was right around the corner, and cards were beginning to flow to our home. One day, while helping Mom hang them on pretty strips of ribbon, I saw one that caught my eye. It was a sensitive sketch of the Madonna and Christ Child. Suddenly, I was inspired to draw one more entry for the contest. I loved the picture on the card and found myself lost in its beauty as I tried to recapture it.

I worked and worked on the Madonna until I thought I had achieved the same gentle eyes and the same soft smile. Then I drew the Baby. He looked so peaceful, sleeping in his mother's arms. I carefully added shadows, depth, and warmth.

I was thrilled with the results! The picture was much better than my other two had been. I had high hopes for it as I sent it off to the newspaper office.

But as the days went by, I began to lose confidence in myself and in my work. I had been sure that my other pictures would win, but they hadn't. Negative thoughts began to creep in. "I could be in for another letdown," I thought. I found myself reluctantly facing Sunday and its results.

The day came, and the sun awakened me with the thought, "Today's your day! Get up and see what it has in store for you!"

Rather than jumping excitedly from my bed, I lay there, arguing with myself.

"What if I lost again? I don't think I can stand it if my picture isn't there!"

"But, on the other hand, maybe you've won! You

must think positively!"

The shafts of sunlight now fell across my bed. The songs of the awakening birds filled me with the wonder of a new day and the new surprises it held for me. Suddenly I thought, "Maybe I *have* won!"

Eagerly I tiptoed through the sleeping house and past my cat, Muffy, who was curled up peacefully on the living room couch.

As I stepped out into the brisk morning air, with the cold pavement under my bare toes, I picked up the newspaper with fresh excitement. I felt the warmth of the sun's rays on my shoulders as I sat down in the middle of the driveway. Giving a hopeful glance to my friend in the eastern sky, I opened the paper with renewed faith. My heart beat stronger with each page I turned. Finally, there it was. I saw the picture in the upper corner, a pretty sketch of the Madonna and her Child. Under it was this caption: "Artist, Sheila Schuller, age eleven."

I had won! Me! Sheila Schuller! My delighted screams pierced the stillness of the morning and awakened the whole house. Poor Muffy—her hair stood straight on end, and she ran for cover as I bounded into the house. Dad jumped out of bed, expecting a major disaster, and baby Jeanne began to cry.

Dad, with hair disheveled and eyes thick with sleep, emerged from the hall and bellowed, "What in the world is going on?"

I threw my arms around him and pushed the

newspaper excitedly in his face. "I won, Dad! I won!"

"Why, Sheila," he said with sleepy enthusiasm. "That's fantastic! I knew you could do it!"

Later that morning I sat in church with Mom. Dad was talking about positive thinking and never giving up. All of a sudden, I realized he was talking about me! He was telling everyone how I had tried and tried and finally won! I was thrilled and proud to be used as a part of Dad's message, and I felt a special little tingle as I realized that the picture that had won had been of Jesus.

From that moment on I was an ardent believer. I firmly believed that if I thought positively enough I could do anything! My interpretation of positive thinking, however, varied from that of Dad. In my childish mind I began to equate positive thinking with magic. I thought that it was as easy as saying, "I think I can," and presto, I would get my way. Well, my magical balloon of "positive thinking" was soon to burst.

It happened one summer when Dad took all of us to a friend's cabin in Minnesota. The bright red cabin was nestled on the plush, green shores of one of that state's thousand lakes, so Dad was anxiously looking forward to lots and lots of fishing. I, personally, couldn't see what was so exciting about fishing. In my opinion, it was just about the most boring thing to do.

Dad, the fisherman, objected. "Sheila," he said, "The only reason you get bored is because you don't catch any fish. You come with me and I'll show you *real* fishing!"

I agreed to give it one more try. So, Dad packed up the boat with all the things he thought we'd need while Bobby and I gathered our own brand of necessities. Mine were bottles of mosquito repellent and bundles of warm sweaters, whereas Bobby's were bags of goodies to eat. Finally, we were off. The oars of the little rowboat silently pulled us across the lake to a tiny cove where we hoped hungry fish were waiting.

Dad quickly threaded the worm along my hook and cast it out over the clear, blue water. "That's the last time I'll bait your hook for you," he warned. "You can catch the limit if you want, but the rules are, 'You bait your own hook.'"

"Okay, Dad," I agreed and then settled back for what I was sure would be a *long* wait.

My hook, however, was barely in the water when I felt a sharp tug on my line. "A fish!" I screamed as I jumped up, nearly dumping all of us into the lake.

"Sheila! Sit down! You want us all to drown?" Dad had a legitimate concern, for the boat was now rocking wildly, and he had never learned how to swim.

I reeled in my line as fast as I could, with visions of a huge fish dangling below. But when I came to the end of my line, all that was there was the worm, dripping, soggy, and hanging on for dear life.

He was a sad-looking worm. Not at all the kind of bait that would lure a big fish. "Should I change him, Dad?" I innocently asked.

Dad, only teasing, replied, "I don't know. Is he wet?"

I looked at the sopping worm and was just about to reply with, "Of course, he is!" when I saw the twinkle in Dad's eye.

Bobby got a good laugh at that. He was feeling pretty smug as it was, with all of his vast fishing experience.

Before I could cast off again, Dad's pole suddenly bent in half. He was the one who was shouting now! After a short struggle, Dad jerked the pole into the air and a shimmering bass flopped into our boat.

Now, Bobby and I began to get our hopes up. Sure enough, before five minutes had passed, both of us had landed a fish.

"Boy, the fish are biting today!" Bobby declared. "They're even going for Sheila's line!"

It was true. The fish were biting. Every time one of us lowered a line into the water, he came up with a fish less than five minutes later.

In no time we had caught our limit and were headed back to the cabin. The sun was setting on the lake behind us as we docked the boat. I had thoroughly enjoyed fishing, and I had a new goal. I wanted to catch one particular fish that week: a ten-pound bass. I knew I could do it; after all, I knew the magic words: *Positive Thinking*!

I spent the remaining six days of our vacation on the

pier, fishing pole in hand, saying over and over, "I think I can! I think I can! I *will* catch a ten-pound bass! I *will* catch a ten-pound bass!"

But after five days, I had not managed to catch a fish even close to ten pounds. Finally, on our last day, while I was standing in my usual place with my usual pole and bait, I suddenly felt a really big tug on the end of my line. It lurched so hard that I thought surely my pole would break. I reeled and reeled with all my might. I was so excited! I could tell I had a really big one! Positive thinking had paid off.

As I fought the big fish, I could see his tail flashing in the sun as he thrashed wildly in the lake. Just as he got within yards of the pier, I threw my pole back with a jerk; and there, flapping on the pier at my feet, was the biggest fish I'd ever seen.

"Daddy!" I called. "Daddy, come quick! I've caught him! I've caught my fish!"

Dad came running from the cabin, with Bobby close on his heels. "Boy, Sheila! He is *big*!" Dad said proudly.

Bobby's eyes were fairly popping out of his head, but all he said was, "I've seen bigger."

I just ignored him. "Let's measure him, Daddy!" Since I had used positive thinking, I knew that my fish would weigh in at ten pounds exactly.

When he lay there on the scale, however, very pathetic looking, no longer the fighting king but only a dead, smelly fish, he weighed only five pounds. Only half as much as I had hoped for!

At that moment I became a skeptic. "Positive

thinking doesn't work!" I declared. "Nobody ever thought more positively than I did that I would catch a ten-pound bass, and all I caught was this stupid five-pound fish!"

"Sheila," Dad quickly responded, "Positive thinking isn't a magic wand that you wave around a certain number of times and expect easy, instant, exact results. Positive thinking is an attitude! It says, 'I won't give up! I'll try harder!' Remember the picture you drew for the newspaper contest last year? You didn't win with your first entry. Your second didn't win either. But the *third* picture came in first place! Why? Because you used positive thinking and didn't give up.

"Look at this fish! Why, he's the biggest one you've ever caught! You never would have caught such a beautiful, big bass if you hadn't thought positively and tried so hard."

Suddenly it sank in. Although my magic balloon had burst, it had given birth to the concept Dad had been trying to teach me all along. Positive thinking isn't easy. In fact, it takes more work to be positive than to be negative. And even if it doesn't make *all* your dreams come true, it will *always* help you make the most of your dreams!

6

Grins, Bears, Mice 'n' Things

From somewhere far away, I felt a gentle rocking and heard my name being called, "Sheila, Sheila."

But I didn't want to be disturbed. "Go away," I murmured as I pulled the covers up around my ears.

But the voice was persistent, growing louder, "Sheila, wake up! It's time to go to Iowa!"

"Iowa?" I had almost forgotten that today was the day we'd leave for Grandpa and Grandma's!

Mom and Dad had already packed the car. Now they gathered a sleepy Bobby, Jeannie, and me, and stuffed us, with pillows and games, into the backseat.

"Join hands, everyone," Dad said as he did every year at the start of our vacation. He turned around in the front seat, as did Mom. We all held hands and prayed silently along with Dad, "Dear Lord, as we begin

this trip, we ask that You will keep us safe from harm
and accident."

"Whew!" I thought. "I'm so glad Daddy always does
that—even before we pull out of the driveway!"

"Dad," I said, "Maybe next year you should pray
that Bobby and Jeanne won't fight all the way to Iowa."

"Well, maybe I should pray that He'll keep Bobby
and *you* from fighting!" he said as he saw Bob reach
around Jeanne and poke me with his chubby, little hand.

We varied our route to Iowa each summer. Some years
we took the hot, grueling trips through Arizona, New
Mexico, and Texas. When Jeanne was a baby, Mom
draped diapers in the windows to keep the hot sun from
glaring in on her sleeping infant. Oh, for the comforts of
air-conditioning! But not in those days.

We did get an air-cooler one year that we fed dry ice
to all the way across the desert. Of course, this proved to
be another source of irritation for Bobby and me. We
both loved being the ice-keeper, because we not only had
the fun of watching the ice vapors creep along the front
seat, but we were also able to hog all the cold air.

Other summers we took a northern route. We'd go
up through the redwoods, Yellowstone Park, and then
cut across the states bordering Canada. Whichever route
we took, we ate all our meals in roadside parks. Those
were some of the best meals I've ever had and some of
the most exciting adventures as well.

There was one adventure in particular I'll never
forget! We had left our motel up north where we had
spent the night and were driving through a gorgeous

forest. The morning light was filtering through the few spaces left by the leaves. The trees sped by the car, leaving glistening streaks before my face, which was pressed to the window.

In spite of the beauty of the sparkling new day, my stomach began to gurgle. "I'm hungry!" I declared. "When can we eat?"

"Pretty soon, Sheila. Start looking for a place."

I'm afraid my bodily instincts took over and distracted me from our beautiful surroundings. I no longer noticed God's spectacular creations, bathed in the morning light. Rather, I looked frantically for one of man's inventions: a park bench. Suddenly I spotted one. "There's one!" I cried as I almost knocked Dad's glasses off with my pointing arm.

"No, Sheila. It's too close to the road. I'd like to wait and find one further away from the noise and the traffic."

"Oh, no," I groaned as my stomach signaled even more furiously.

After what seemed like an eternity of "too-close-to-the-road" benches, Dad finally said, "Here's a sign, 'Picnic turn-out ahead.' That should be what we're looking for."

As soon as we pulled into the pretty little nook, we all felt grateful to Dad for waiting until we'd found the perfect place.

"Oh, Bob!" Mom sighed. "It's beautiful!"

I had to agree. It was worth the wait. Not only was the sheltered clearing quiet and peaceful, but it also

backed up against a bubbly, clear brook. This was just
the right place for breakfast.

As we sprang from the car, I dragged Dad by the
arm, saying, "Oh, Daddy! Look at that pretty stream!
Can we go wading?"

"Yes, but stay close enough that Mom and I can see
you at all times."

"Okay," I hastily agreed. And Bobby, Jeanne, and I
were off like a shot. We quickly pulled off our shoes and
socks, rolled up our pantlegs, and soon felt the smooth,
slippery stones under our toes. The cool, rushing
springwater made our legs tingle with the morning chill.

Bobby had to splash everyone, of course, until Dad
came. "Now, Robert! That's enough! I don't want to
have wet kids riding in the car all the way to Iowa!"

But Bobby had to get one more in. He scooped up a
handful of water and threw it right at Jeanne. As she
desperately tried to dodge the water, her little feet
slipped on the slick pebbles and, boom, down she went.

She immediately let out a shrill cry. Only a few
seconds later Dad rescued her from the ice-cold pool.
With a dripping Jeanne held tightly in his arms, Dad
said, "It's okay, Jeanne. I've got you."

He shot Bobby a "sermon-in-a-glance" as he carried
Jeannie back to the warm campfire.

Once I saw that she was all right, I began to laugh. She
did look pretty funny. Then Daddy started to laugh, and
finally, Jeanne, with tears still shimmering in her eyes,
laughed, too.

Our moment of mirth was interrupted by the dinner

bell. "Come and get it, everyone!" Mom called.

Wow! All of a sudden I could smell the terrific scent of bacon and eggs riding down the cool, morning breeze.

"Mmmm, bacon and eggs! I almost forgot! I'm starved!"

I don't think any food ever looked better or smelled as yummy as breakfast did that morning. I scurried to my seat and watched, drooling, as Mom put two eggs and three slices of bacon on my plate. Just as my plate was about to be passed to me, suddenly, and to my horror, Mom threw it in the air and screamed, "Bob! A bear!"

Before I could mourn my destroyed breakfast for very long, Dad had grabbed my hand, snatched up the still-wet Jeanne, and run to the car, pulling me along after him. I stumbled a little as I turned around to see if Mommy and Bobby were coming, too.

"A real, live bear?" he was asking eagerly. "Where?"

"Never mind!" Mom said sharply (which she rarely did). "Come on!" She dragged my brother, who was still returning the stare of the bear that was partly hidden by the bushes.

My heart was beating wildly as I watched the bear lumber out of his not-so-hidden hiding place. He was following his nose which had latched onto the same wonderful wafting scents that had lured me to the table. He was headed right for my bacon and eggs!

"Oh, no! There goes my breakfast! My delicious breakfast! And I'm sooo hungry!" I wailed.

But all we could do was sit behind our locked doors

and watch helplessly as that lazy bear devoured all of
Mom's hard work—our delicious breakfast. After he'd
made an absolute pig of himself, and an absolute mess of
our picnic, he turned and walked, oh, so slowly, back to
the forest. After he had been swallowed up by the trees,
we sat breathlessly and waited. Finally, when Dad was
sure that he had gone, he said, "Okay, let's go and gather
our things just as fast as we can and get out of here.
Jeanne, you stay right here! Don't move!"

As quick as beavers, we gathered up our belongings,
dumped them in the car, and left the once-peaceful, now
battle-torn glade in a cloud of dust.

It wasn't until we were a good five minutes away that I
felt my pants starting to get damp. Jeannie, still wet from her
fall was sitting next to me. We had left in such a hurry that
we had packed up everything just as it was, and that included
a soggy Jeanne. Fortunately, there was a restaurant not far
away.

Those summer days on the road to Iowa were
fantastic! I always had so much fun! But being the
impatient child that I was, I was always eager to reach
our destination. Mom and Dad were certainly very
patient with my constant queries of, "How much farther
to Iowa?" And once we hit Iowa, "How much farther to
Grandpa's?" And finally, "Aren't we there yet?"

An Iowan farm is a child's dream come true. There are
newborn calves to feed, eggs to gather, baby kittens to
stroke, old, faithful dogs to play with, trees to climb,
pastures to run in, tractors to ride, attics to explore, and

haylofts to conquer, jumping from bale to bale.

And, oh, the food! Grandma's raisin bread toasting in the morning would always lure me downstairs. Lunches in Iowa are virtual feasts! We had meat and potatoes, vegetables, and always dessert. Grandma's apple pies were piled so high with her homegrown crab apples that they could barely stand up.

One morning I quietly came around the corner into Grandma's kitchen. I was looking for my usual raisin toast but, instead, I discovered Dad. There he sat with the biggest piece of apple pie I'd ever seen.

"Dad! Are you eating that *before* breakfast?"

Startled, he looked up with that same guilty look of a young boy caught with his hand in the cookie jar. But this time it was worse than cookies! It was apple pie— and the first thing in the morning at that! I really can't blame him. Grandma's pies were irresistible!

After we'd been in Iowa for about a month and enjoyed all the cousins, aunts, and uncles, we'd head back to California—usually ten pounds heavier!

The trip home was never as exciting as the trip out to Iowa. It was always hard to leave our loved ones, knowing it would be another year before we'd see them again. Usually, the route home was the shortest and the least exciting—straight through the desert.

We always had our share of car troubles. These were always major emergencies, because if there's one thing Dad isn't, it's mechanical. However gifted he may be in other areas of life, he is just that *un*gifted when it comes to fixing things.

So when our car, sailing along the deserted desert road, suddenly began to bump and bounce uncontrollably, we knew we were in trouble. Sure enough, it was a flat tire. It was, of course, excruciatingly hot, and we were out in the middle of nowhere.

"Don't panic! I'll take care of it," Dad reassured us. But when he got the jack out and couldn't figure out how to use it, it was difficult to stay optimistic. Even Dad had trouble being positive that day.

He tried the jack in many different positions, most of which were pretty compromising. But none of them worked. He was getting more and more frustrated by the minute, and finally, the frayed nerves became easily ignited by the intense heat of the desert sun. Dad exploded, "I *can't* do it. This jack is impossible to figure out! What good is an emergency kit, when it takes a mechanical genius to figure it out? And, obviously, there wouldn't be an emergency if there were a mechanical genius around, now would there?"

I choked back the phrases that immediately popped into my head, like, ". . . the difficult you do immediately, the impossible just takes a little longer."

Instead, I managed a weak, "What now, Dad?" I was beginning to have visions of Mom, Bob, and me gathering up cactus leaves for dinner.

Dad looked at our stricken faces and quickly calmed down. "Don't worry. 'Where there's a will, there's a way.' Who says that the only way you can change a tire is with a jack?"

He suddenly got in the car and pulled it off the road

so that the flat tire was well in the sand. Before I knew what was happening, Dad was sitting in the sand, tire between his legs, and starting to dig. He dug and dug, calling frequently for more water to drink. We were all hot, but poor Dad was on the verge of sunstroke.

After about a half hour of this digging, Dad ran into another challenge. "Great!" he said sarcastically. "A whole desert of nothing but sand, and I pick the one stone in the state to park over!"

I peered over Dad's dirty, sweaty shoulder and saw in the hole, right under our flat tire, a huge stone. "Here, Dad, let us help!" I said; and Mom and Bobby and I helped Dad wiggle and wiggle the big rock until it finally was worked loose.

When Dad lifted it out, I could suddenly see what he was doing, for now there was a huge hole right under the drooping tire, leaving plenty of room to pull it off and put on the spare.

I was never so relieved to get back on the road and pull into our driveway, late that night.

Dad's method may have been unconventional, but it worked. I think that's part of his success today. He certainly doesn't suffer from locked-in thinking. He's always looking for new and different ways to do things, such as catching a mouse.

Dad had taken all of us to the cabin that he had built for Mom in the mountains. He knew how hard Mom worked, so he had a cabin built as a place of rest and relaxation for her. The only problem was, the cabin was so wonderful that all of us kids usually tagged along, bringing our friends, our dogs, our water skis, and general pandemonium with us.

I'm afraid that most of the time, Mom had more work in her "relaxing" cabin than she did at home. But I also know she loved it.

This particular day was one in a typical summer. We had brought some friends with us and, having worn each other out, settled down for a night of sleep. Finally, after a long, tiring day, Mom, too, was able to go to bed. Just as she was drifting off, she heard a scuffle in the closet. Mom knew the sound. She was suddenly fully awake. "Bob!" she said as she awakened Dad, "There's a mouse in here!"

Dad just yawned and said, "Now, Arvella, there's nothing to be afraid of. Just go to sleep."

"I can't! Please, can't you get up and get rid of him?"

Dad wasn't about to get out of bed just for a silly old mouse. He laughed and said, "Arvella, you're not afraid of a little mouse, are you?"

"If you're so brave, then why don't you get out of this bed and go get him?" she retorted.

"Okay," he said, still laughing.

He went to the hall closet and got a broom. Like a warrior stalking the enemy, Dad crept through the room in his shorts, his hair tousled, broom raised over his head, poised for battle.

Mom acted as general from her post in the middle of the bed. All of a sudden she shrieked, "There he goes!"

"Where?"

Mom was pointing wildly, "There! There!"

Dad suddenly spotted the mouse and began chasing him, beating his broom first this way and then that way.

"I just saw him go into the kitchen," Mom shouted.

Dad and his broom came running after the mouse. He saw it run for cover behind the stove. Dad, the triumphant warrior, declared, "I've got him now!"

That poor mouse should have been scared to death. Here came Dr. Schuller, an imposing man in his sleepwear, on hands and knees peering under the stove. Just as he had the mouse in his sights and had drawn the broom back for its fatal blow, that mighty mouse drew a deep breath and lunged right at Dad's face!

We were awakened by horrible whacks, crashes, screams, and Mom's hysterical laughter. As we all came running out of our rooms, Dad yelled, "Go back! Go back! I'm not dressed!"

An important lesson that Dad has taught us is that humor is the honey of life. Sometimes, like apple pie in the morning, it's nice, although not essential. Other times, after being dunked in a stream or losing one's breakfast to a bear, it "helps the medicine go down." At those times it can be the best healing ointment in the world.

One of the best things about Dad is that he can always dish out the laughter in BIG doses!

7

Green Doughnuts

I was just about to walk into the living room when low, secretive voices stopped me.

"What do you think, Bob?" I recognized Mom's voice. "Do you think we should buy that house?"

I didn't even wait for Dad's reply. I had heard all I wanted to hear.

I walked back to my room in a daze. "New house? They can't mean it! Why, we've lived here for eight years. All my friends are here and all my memories, too."

I lay back on my bed and slowly surveyed my pretty room. Mom and I had just finished decorating it. I loved the rose wallpaper that we had picked out together. My eyes followed the lines of roses and finally settled on one particular blossom. Its petals softly faded and dissolved until they formed a delicate frame for my memories.

The first picture that came into focus was of Dad. He was holding a kite in his hand and calling, "Run, Sheila! Run!" I turned and ran as fast as my legs could carry me until I felt the string go taut as the evening breeze caught and carried my kite high into the sky.

Then I could see Grandpa. He was carrying wood over to our tree. I was watching eagerly as he put the finishing touches on my brand-new tree house.

My tree house was a source of many happy memories. It was the favorite lunch site for my friends—Cindy and Georgina—and me. Since I lived only a block from Faylane Elementary School, we were able to sneak home to my backyard, hide in the tree house, and eat our sack lunches in luxurious seclusion. Suspended high above the world by the tree's strong branches and hidden by the living wall of leaves, we were in our glory.

We managed to keep our lunch rendezvous a secret until one day I spoiled it all by my need to show off. There was a bush near our home that housed a hive of "H-bees." These are yellow flies with black "H's" on their backs. They look just like bees, if a person doesn't know better, except they don't sting.

Since Cindy and Georgina didn't know what "H-bees" were, I boasted, "I can catch bees in my bare hands!"

"Oh, you can't!"

"I can, too!"

"Oh, yeah? Let's see."

The challenge was just what I was waiting for, so I courageously went up to the bush that was aswarm with bees, carefully cupped my hands around them, and carried them back to my wide-eyed friends.

"I could feel the soft creatures buzzing around in my palms, but I knew they wouldn't sting me. "Do you hear them?" I asked.

"Sure can! Gosh! How did you do that?"

I explained the phenomena of "H-Bees," which prompted Cindy and Georgina to bravely catch a few, too.

"Hey! I've got an idea!" I said suddenly. "Let's catch a whole bag of these bees and take 'em back to school with us!"

"That's a great idea!" said Georgina.

"Yeah! It sounds like fun!" said Cindy.

We filled our empty lunch bags with buzzing bees and brazenly scared most of the school yard.

Instead of letting them go when the bell rang, we rolled over the tops of the bags and took them into the classroom with us.

Everything was going smoothly enough, until the boy sitting directly behind Georgina accidentally kicked over her bag of bees. Suddenly, bees were flying everywhere. Girls started screaming and jumping out of their seats, desperately trying to avoid them. In the frenzy, Cindy's bag tipped over and so did mine.

Mr. Leach, our teacher, became outraged. "GEOR-

GI-NA!" he called. "Come to my desk immediately!"

But I leaped to Georgina's defense. After all, it had been my idea. "Mr. Leach! It's okay. There's no need for everyone to get so upset!"

But as a bee flew past Mr. Leach's face, he recoiled and demanded nervously, "N-NO NEED?"

I hastily explained, "No, Sir. You see, these bees don't sting."

But no one believed me. "I don't care if they sting or not! Just get them out of here! NOW!"

I'm surprised that Mr. Leach didn't have us expelled right then and there. He did, however, find out about our tree-house lunches and promptly put a stop to them.

Mom suddenly broke into my reminiscing with a call for dinner. The room came back into focus as I remembered the conversation I'd overheard. "We can't move! We just can't!"

I'm afraid I wasn't my bubbly self as I helped out in the kitchen that night. Mom didn't say anything that even remotely suggested a move, and not a hint of it was made at dinner. I figured that for some reason Mom and Dad were trying to keep it a big secret.

After dinner I helped with dishes as usual. This particular night, as I was putting away a mixing bowl, my attention was caught by a jar of green food coloring. My memory was immediately aroused. Although I continued to dry the dishes, my mind had returned to my fifth grade class.

Mr. Leach had given me the project of the

Christmas bulletin board. I was thrilled and honored. I even went in early every day to work on it. (That was a miracle for me. I never have been able to get anywhere on time, much less *early*!)

I decided to make a huge Christmas tree and decorate it with all kinds of ornaments. I spent hours on each star, snowflake, and candy cane in an attempt to make my tree something special. I was very proud of my work and was almost done when I decided to add some miniature wreaths. I carefully cut them out of green construction paper and added red holly berries.

I had just finished putting together the last wreath when I hastily glanced at the clock. I still had a few minutes before class was to start, so I quickly pulled up a chair and pinned a wreath somewhere between an angel and a snowflake. Suddenly Billy, one of my classmates, said loudly, "Hey, Sheila! What'cha puttin' up there? Green doughnuts?"

My classmates thought that was pretty funny. I felt my face grow hot as I stood perched on a chair in front of all of them. I had three more "green doughnuts" in my hand ready to go on the board.

I wasn't about to let Billy get the best of me. I retorted as I pinned up another wreath, "Why, Billy, haven't you ever seen a green doughnut before?"

"There's no such thing, Sheila, and you know it!"

"Oh, yeah?" I continued, defensively, "I've seen plenty of green doughnuts."

"I'll believe it when I see it!"

Mr. Leach came in just then, and I scurried to my

seat. I barely heard a word of the "Pledge of Allegiance" or any of the other school lessons, for my mind was preoccupied with green doughnuts. I couldn't wait to get home where I could be alone. "Why did I have to be so doggone proud and have to challenge Billy like that?" I asked myself, over and over.

I ran home as soon as the final bell had rung. "Mom!" I called as I ran into the house. "Where are you?"

"I'm out here!" she called from the kitchen. "How was school today?"

"Oh, Mom. I've never been so embarrassed in all my life," I said as I let myself cry for the first time that day.

"Come, Sheila. Sit down and tell me all about it."

The story of the wreaths and green doughnuts came out bit by bit between sobs. Finally, I said, "I feel so stupid! Everyone knows that there's no such thing as a green doughnut!"

"Who says?" she asked.

Surprised, I looked up into Mom's face. Although she appeared blurred through my tear-filled eyes, I recognized that familiar look of determination.

"I think I can find you a green doughnut," she continued.

"N-no kidding?"

"No kidding! You know what Daddy says. 'Use possibility thinking and some imagination and you can solve any problem!' Finding a green doughnut will just take a little possibility thinking and a little imagination, that's all. Just leave it to me."

I believed Mom totally. Boy, would Billy be surprised when he showed up at school tomorrow—only to be presented with a real green doughnut!

True to her word, Mom left Bobby, Jeanne, and me in Daddy's care as soon as dinner was over. "I'll be right back. I'm going shopping for a green doughnut."

But she didn't come right back. She was gone for hours. Finally, Daddy said, "Sheila, it's past your bedtime. You can't wait up for Mommy any longer."

"Oh, Daddy! I have to see if Mommy found my green doughnut first."

Just then Mom came bursting through the front door, a shopping bag in her arms. "Sheila! What are you doing up?"

"I was waiting for you."

She looked down at me tenderly and said, "Sheila, I've been to every doughnut shop in the city. I couldn't find a single green doughnut."

As my face registered my deep disappointment, she quickly added, "But, don't forget what I said earlier. Do you remember? 'Use a little bit of possibility thinking and a little bit of imagination.' Well, that's just what I did.

"I figure if I take these plain doughnuts, make some icing out of this powdered sugar, mix it with some of this green food coloring and top it off with red-hot 'holly berries,' we'll have ourselves a terrific-looking green doughnut!

"Now, come. Let me tuck you into bed and hear your prayers."

I snuggled down deep under the covers and prayed confidently as I felt Mom's hand gently stroke my cheek. "And, dear God," I concluded, "Bless Billy and my green doughnut."

The next morning I dashed expectantly into the kitchen. Mom was fixing breakfast.

"Good morning, Sheila! Well, what do you think?" she asked as she pointed to the table. There on my plate was a box, and in it was a doughnut, glazed with green icing and red hots scattered here and there. It looked exactly like the wreaths I had pinned on the bulletin board.

"It's terrific! Thanks, Mom!" I said with a big hug and kiss.

"You're welcome, Sheila. Now, go get ready for school."

I couldn't wait! I played the scene over and over in my mind. Boy, was Billy going to be surprised.

I purposefully got to school early and strategically hid the box in my desk. Then, as Mr. Leach started class, I raised my hand.

"Yes, Sheila?"

My heart started beating wildly. "I have a presentation to make, if I may, Mr. Leach."

"Oh? Well, I suppose that will be all right."

I took a big gulp and said, "Yesterday, I was told

that I was putting green doughnuts on my bulletin board."

I looked squarely at Billy. He was the one who looked embarrassed now. "And, I was told that there is no such thing as a green doughnut. Well, to prove that there are, I have brought, for Billy, a green doughnut!"

I ceremoniously presented my box with its unique contents to Billy. He looked in and then grinned sheepishly at me.

Billy and I both had a good laugh, and everyone applauded. It was a great success.

As the memories of the applause died down and the faces of my classmates faded away, I looked at the bottle of green food coloring on the shelf. "What a great day," I thought. But then I remembered Mom's words and realized, "It'll be hard to move and leave all my friends, but I can handle any challenge if I only use a little bit of possibility thinking and a little bit of imagination. Who knows what adventures await me in our new house?"

8

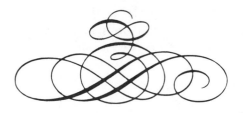

Gain Through Pain

I looked at my newly completed painting with dismay. "This looks awful!" I thought. It didn't look anything like the picture I had painted in my mind; but it was too late to do anything about it anymore today, for class was just about over.

Sure enough, the bell rang just as I cleaned out my last brush. I rushed out into the crowded corridor and looked frantically for Ann, the one friend that I had made since we had moved and I had entered the new junior high school. I felt frightened by the sea of strange faces that pushed past me. Finally, to my relief, I spotted her.

"Ann!" I cried out as I waved over the masses.

Her smile soothed me. "How was art?" she asked.

"Awful! How was beginning orchestra?"

"Oh, Sheila! I love it! Violin is so much fun, and Mr. Schmidt is teaching us so much!"

I recalled my miserable experience with painting and compared it to Ann's exhilarating experience in violin. "I sure wish I had signed up for beginning orchestra with you."

"It's not too late. Today's the deadline for registration changes. If we go to the office right after school, I'll bet you could still get in."

"But what about a violin? I don't have one, and I know Mom and Dad can't afford one now, not after they just bought a new house and all."

"That's okay. They have instruments that you can check out to practice on."

That settled it. "Violin, here I come!"

I loved my first lesson and checked out a violin the very first night. "This will be fun. It won't be nearly as frustrating as that stupid art class," I foolishly thought.

As soon as I got home, I retreated to my room, anxious to put Mr. Schmidt's demonstration into practice.

"Let's see. This should be pretty easy," I said as I unpacked the delicate instrument. "All I have to do is first, pick up the violin—like so. Then second, pick up the bow— like so. So far, so good. Now, all I have to do is draw the bow across the strings—like so."

I began to bow and bow with all the finesse of a maestro, or so I thought. But, unfortunately, the sounds that came out were not that of a maestro, but rather they were squawks that sounded like fingernails being dragged across a chalkboard.

I had barely begun when Mom came bursting into the room, "What in the world . . . " she started to ask, but she stopped short when she saw my new passion tucked lovingly under my chin. "Why, Sheila! V-violin! You didn't tell me you were going to start lessons."

"I know. It was supposed to be a surprise. I know how much you love the violin, and since lessons are free at school, I decided to transfer from art to beginning orchestra."

"Oh? H-have you already made the switch?" she asked with a touch of apprehension.

*Portrait of an apprentice
possibility thinker.*

"Oh, yes. I made it just in time. Today was the last day to make transfers. Isn't that fortunate?"

"Y-yes. Th-that's very fortunate," she gulped.

Beginning orchestra was my favorite part of the day. I could hardly wait to get through the rest of my classes so that I could go and learn more about the violin. And every afternoon I raced home to spend hours in my room, practicing the exercises over and over. When I lovingly caressed the strings with long, sweeping strokes of the bow, the tones that flowed forth were like velvet to my ears. However, no one else seemed to think so.

One day, all my practicing paid off. Mr. Schmidt invited me to join the advanced orchestra. I couldn't believe it!

My first rehearsal with the other instrumentalists was exciting. I was intrigued by the intricate way all the different instruments fit together to make a big, colorful picture.

But my first day was also just as frustrating as it was exciting. From the minute Mr. Schmidt put music in front of me, I was lost. I couldn't tell what page we were on, much less what measure.

Meanwhile, the "pros" in the upper section were furiously playing their violins, and were they good! One boy in particular was excellent. He had studied for five years. He could play anything.

"I sure wish I could play like him!" I thought as I desperately counted rests and looked for my notes.

After a week of my playing "hunt and seek" during

rehearsal, Mr. Schmidt stood up and made an announcement. "Next Wednesday is the day for our next challenge. Anyone wishing to enter must sign up by Friday. Class dismissed."

I turned quickly to the girl next to me. She'd been in orchestra a lot longer than I had. "Excuse me," I said over the din of fifty students packing up instruments. "What's a 'challenge'?"

" 'A challenge'?" She stood up from where she was bent over her violin case. "That's where anyone who wants can challenge any player for his seat in the orchestra. The two players perform behind that screen up there, and everyone votes. The winner gets the seat assignment."

That night I announced at the dinner table that I was going to challenge that same girl for her seat in orchestra.

Dad was very supportive. "I think that's great, Sheila! Everyone should have a goal. No one gets ahead unless he sets goals that require extra work to reach."

I gave violin every bit of extra effort and work that I could. I was determined to win. I practiced night and day, while Mom and Dad patiently endured and even encouraged me.

The morning of the challenges found me fully prepared but scared to death. Dad took me to school that day as he did every day. I sat in the front seat, nervously fingering the case of my instrument.

"You'll do great today, Sheila!" Dad said enthusiastically.

"You think so?" I desperately needed reassurance.

"Sure! You've worked hard, and now the only thing you need to do is to remember to use positive thinking. Imagine yourself as the best violin player in the whole world. That will free you to do your best. And after all— that's all that matters."

"Okay, Dad, I'll remember to use positive thinking." I didn't want to disappoint him. But most of all, I didn't want to disappoint me.

Since the challenges were held at the end of the school day, I had to sit nervously through algebra, history, English, and biology. I didn't hear a word my teachers said that day, and my hands shook so uncontrollably in biology that I almost dissected my finger instead of the frog.

Finally, the time came. I, the challenger, and she, the challenged, stood behind the screen. She played first. Her performance was beautiful. Now it was my turn. I took my violin and bow and raised them to their familiar pose. I closed my eyes for a second and imagined myself as the best violin player in the world. Then I took a deep breath, and I let my practiced fingers fly from position to position.

I felt wonderful. I felt in total control. I played the selection better than I ever had.

Before I knew it, it was all over. Mr. Schmidt asked the class to vote, and then he announced the winner— me!

I had reached my goal! I raced home to share the

good news with Mom and Dad. They were so proud of
me.

"Dad," I exclaimed when he came home that night,
"I did it! I imagined myself as the best violin player, and
then I played my very best! And guess what? I won!"

"That's terrific, Sheila! I knew you could do it!"

"Yes, and I'm going to keep challenging the other
players until I'm first chair, concert master of advanced
orchestra!"

"Good for you! Every time you challenge, you will
be motivated to practice that much more; and,
consequently, you'll be that much better as a violin
player and as a young adult."

And so, chair by chair, I challenged my way to the
top of the orchestra. I met each individual goal with
determination and hard work, so that one year later I
had reached my ultimate goal. I became first chair violin,
concert master of the orchestra.

I saw that by taking one large, impossible goal and
breaking it into small, possible goals, I could do
anything!

Goal-setting is very important in my family. Dad has
often said, "It's not the goal that's important, but it's
what the goal does for you."

My parents encouraged me to follow my childhood
dream of being a doctor. That dream, they reasoned,
would develop character within me. Although I changed
my goal later, the character that it developed within me

has stayed with me my entire life.

As important as goals were during my growing, and sometimes groping, junior high years, so also was parental involvement. Some may call it "parental intrusion"; but as far as I'm concerned, I'm deeply grateful that they cared enough to step in.

We hadn't been living in our new home for very long when the twins, Sarah and Sally, moved nearby. "Girls my age," I thought. "This is great! Two new friends at once."

I hit it off with them immediately. They were just as glad as I to find a new friend. They were spunky, with a slightly naughty streak, but I enjoyed the sense of adventure that I felt whenever I was with them. One day, though, we became involved in an adventure that I could very well have done without.

We had been walking home from school as we did everyday. This particular day was a scorcher. The walk was long; there were very few trees along the way, and my schoolbooks began to cause pools of perspiration in the crook of my elbow. I was hot!

Sarah suggested, "Hey, let's stop for a minute in that store and cool off."

"That sounds good," I sighed.

The cold air from the store was an icy blast compared to the hot sun. I wandered around from section to section, being refreshed by the cool refrigeration.

All of a sudden I came to the ice-cream section. I love ice cream. And on that hot day, the ice-cream sandwiches looked *so* tempting!

Sally sidled up next to me; and seeing the drool in my eyes, she asked with a mask of innocence, "Do you want it?"

"Oh, yes! It looks *so* good, and I'm *so* hot!"

"If you want it, then take it," she hissed.

"Take it? You mean steal?" I was appalled! I had never stolen anything in my entire life.

"It's easy, Sheila. Look at what you're holding. All you have to do is slip it between your books, and no on will ever be the wiser."

My heart started to pound as I rationalized, "She's right. No one will ever know. And what's a lousy old dime to a store owner who makes millions? Especially, since I could die of heatstroke on the way home."

The next thing I knew, I had slipped the sandwich into my belongings. I hurried out of the store; and once we were well out of sight, I pulled out my "hot" ice-cream sandwich. It was so "hot," in fact, that I couldn't eat it. I felt miserable! How could I eat this sandwich? I had stolen it!

Finally, Sarah taunted, "What's the matter, Sheila? You've got the ice-cream sandwich that you wanted so much. So, how come you're not eating it?"

"It doesn't look very good anymore. You can have it if you want."

Sally and Sarah ate the ice cream delightedly.

They laughed and bubbled all the way, but I felt sicker and sicker the closer I got to home.

Although I tried to come in as quietly as I could, Mom heard me the moment the door opened. "Sheila! Is that you?"

"Yes, Mom," I muttered. I wanted to run to my room and die. But no such luck.

"Come here and tell me all about your day," she called.

I was trapped. There was no getting out of facing Mom; I put on the cheeriest face I could muster.

Apparently, though, it wasn't cheery enough, for Mom saw right through it. "What's wrong, Sheila?"

"Nothing."

"There is, too. I know you and I know that something is definitely wrong."

Since I was about to burst with guilt as it was, all Mom had to do was ask. I instantly "came unglued." Between choking sobs, I cried, "M-M-Mom. I-I'm so awful! I-I'm a failure as a d-daughter!"

Mom quickly put her arms around me. "That's not true, Sheila! That's simply not true!"

"B-but you don't know!" I protested.

"Don't know what?"

"I stole, Mom! I'm a thief!"

"What did you take, Sheila?"

"An ice-cream sandwich. I was *so* hot, and *so* hungry, and. . . ."

"Did Sarah and Sally encourage you to take it?"

"How did you know?"

"Because it's not like you to do things like that. You would only steal something if you were prodded by someone else."

She thought a minute and then looked at me firmly. "Sheila, what you have done is wrong, and you cannot blame it on the twins. Even if they did tempt you, in the final analysis, only one person took that ice-cream sandwich—you. But if this is the kind of influence that they are going to have, and if you cannot stand up to them, then we will have to do something drastic about this."

That was all I heard about the incident until later that afternoon. Dad came home from the office. I was still not completely over my attack of guilt feeling, so I had spent the remainder of the day in my room.

What I didn't know was that Mom had pulled Dad aside and told him everything. Together they made a decision.

Long around five o'clock, the doorbell rang. Since my room was the closest, I volunteered, "I'll get it."

But Dad beat me to it. As I came around the corner in the hall, I could see Dad, partially hidden by the open door. I recognized Sarah's voice. "Can Sheila come over for awhile before dinner?"

By now I was afraid of Sarah. I realized that she was stronger than I was, and I didn't trust myself with her anymore. I found myself hoping that Dad would say, "I'm sorry. It's too late."

Instead, Dad said, "Sarah, Sheila told her mother what happened at the store today. I know it's not totally your fault, but I don't think she would have done this if you hadn't encouraged her. For that reason, I am forbidding her to see you or Sally ever again."

I couldn't believe my ears! "Parents don't tell junior highers who their friends can or can't be!" I reasoned to myself. "And the twins' friendship is important to me." I couldn't afford to lose any friends, not after just moving.

But to my surprise, I was relieved. I knew that Dad was protecting me, and I was suddenly very grateful.

I heard the door close, and I walked out cautiously into the entry where Dad still stood.

"Does this mean that I can't ever see the twins again?"

"That's right."

"That's really not fair, Dad. I mean, I'm the one who stole the sandwich, not them."

"I know that."

"Then, why aren't you punishing me instead of them?"

"Because I know that you are a good girl, Sheila. I know that you always try to do and to be your best at everything. I know that you're not going to be perfect, and I know that sometimes you are going to fail. That's why God gave you parents. He knows that you aren't strong enough to stand all on your own, yet. Someday you will be, but it's up to your mother and me to protect you against the influences that will defeat you before you're able. Does that make sense?"

"I think so." I felt Dad's strong arm wrap around my shoulder as he said, "Come, I think it's time for dinner."

As he led me back into the family room where Mom was putting food on the table, I suddenly felt very loved and secure in my family unit. I knew that Dad would keep a loving eye on me and a protective arm around me, warding off influences against which my own defenses could not yet stand, until the day when I would be strong enough for him to turn me over to the care of my Heavenly Father.

9

New Additions

I tossed restlessly despite the early hour. I plumped the pillows as full as they would go and pulled the sheets up high around my ears. After lying in this position perhaps thirty seconds, I suddenly threw off the covers altogether, discarded the pillows, and stared hopelessly at the ceiling.

Although it was a Saturday morning and I had nowhere to go, here it was only six o'clock, and I was unable to sleep.

After I finished fighting the bed, I finally gave into the new day and listened to its subdued sounds. Outside, the birds were beginning to stir, and the leaves gently brushed against each other. Inside, I could hear only silence coming from Jeanne and Bobby's rooms and an occasional snore from Mom and Dad's.

My reverie was interrupted by the thought, "Wouldn't it be nice to surprise Mom with a sparkling clean kitchen?"

Inspired by the idea, I jumped out of bed, carefully stepped over my discarded pillows, and eagerly tiptoed to the kitchen. My mission was to change the shelf paper and rearrange the pots and pans before anyone else woke up.

As I quietly pulled the pots and pans from the cupboards and piled them around me on the kitchen floor, I dreamed of the look of surprise I was sure Mom would have. Since I didn't know when she'd get up, I was nervous and jumpy. That's why, when out of the silence I heard, "Sheila, what's . . . ?"

But Mom's last words were drowned out by the clanking, clattering pan I had dropped.

"Oh, Mom!" I cried as I scurried to fix the shambles I had created. "I wanted to surprise you with a clean kitchen!"

"Why, Sheila! That's a wonderful thought!"

Just then Dad came running in. "What on earth is going on here?"

"I-I couldn't sleep, so I thought I'd get up and help Mom. I'm sorry I made such a mess and woke you up. I'll clean it up right away."

Dad was touched by my thoughtfulness, and he turned to Mom and said, "Arvella, we're sure going to need a helper like Sheila around here now. Perhaps we'd

_____

better tell her."

"Tell me what?" I asked.

But Mom ignored me as she answered Dad,
"Perhaps you're right." Then she looked me straight in
the eye and joyously nodded her head up and down.

"Yes? Yes, what?" I didn't know what she meant.
And by now I was nearly beside myself with curiosity.

But Mom thought I knew what she was thinking,
for she just kept nodding her head and saying, "Yes,
Sheila! Your suspicions are right!"

Finally it dawned on my fourteen-year-old mind.
My mouth fell open and I said, "Do you mean—you're
going to have—a baby?"

"Yes!" she laughed, "I am!"

I was ecstatic! Another baby! "When, Mom, when?"

"A few weeks before Christmas."

Of course, it wasn't long before the whole church
knew about the upcoming event in the Schuller
household. And it was no secret that we all wanted a
boy. Bob, especially, had all kinds of plans for his little
brother.

At fourteen, I was fascinated by the miracle that was
happening within Mom. The doctor let me hear the
baby's heartbeat at one visit, and Mom let me feel it
kick. Sometimes, the baby kicked so hard that we could
see the outline of its foot.

We all had tremendous fun getting everything in
order. Mom and I pulled out Jeannie's old crib, painted

it, and added decals of soft little lambs and fuzzy little
bunnies.

As the time drew closer, I loved to go and stand by
the crib and imagine how the new baby would look,
wrapped in its soft receiving blanket.

And, finally, on December 4, Mom began acting
funny, and Dad suddenly whisked her off to the hospital.
I couldn't stand the excitement or the waiting.

It seemed like an eternity before Dad came home.
Wearily, he gathered Bobby, Jeannie, and me around
him and said, "Children, today God has given us a new
little Schuller! Today, God has given you a new sister!"

Bob groaned, but Jeanne and I were delighted.

Dad continued, "Your mother and I have decided
that since the baby's birthday is so close to Christmas,
we'll call her Carol. She is our little Christmas Carol sent
to bring us Christmas joy all year long."

I couldn't wait until Mom could bring Carol home.
I was sure that she would be an absolutely beautiful
baby. School dragged by the next three days until, at
last, it was the day of baby Carol's homecoming.

I rushed home from school and quickly checked the
house to make sure that everything was in order. The
diapers were ready, the bottles were ready. Just then I
heard the car.

"Bob! Jeanne! They're here!" All three of us kids
dashed out the front door. There was Mom. I had surely
missed her. She looked radiant, even though she did look
tired. And there was Carol. She was so tiny and so soft.

I spent hours sitting in front of Carol's crib. I was

amazed at her tiny toes and fingers, and every little detail of her.

She was a Christmas joy for us, and she brought wonder and delight to our family.

But no sooner had we taught Carol to say, "Mama" and "Dadda," than "Mama" announced to me one morning that she was expecting *another* baby!

W ell, Carol was fun. But another? What would the kids think at school? By now, I was in high school, so my response to Mom's announcement was an unenthusiastic, "Another baby?"

"Yes, Sheila! Isn't that wonderful?"

When I failed to join in on the excitement, Mom quickly explained. "Dad and I really would like to have another son. We tried for one with Carol; and since she follows Jeanne by so many years, we thought we'd try once more, and, at the same time, we'd give Carol a companion."

That made sense. This time, though, everyone thought we'd better try positive thinking. Whenever anyone referred to the baby Mom was carrying, it was called "Peter John." And every piece of baby clothing we got was blue. Someone even gave us a darling baseball outfit to fit a six-month-old boy.

My initial embarassment quickly turned to eager anticipation. I began to count off the days until "Peter John's" arrival.

About a month before the February date that the

doctor had given Mom, I happened to overhear a crucial
decision. Dad was protesting in his usual vociferous way,
"Arvella, I won't go! They'll understand."

"Now, Bob. This speaking engagement has been on
your calendar for over a year. You can't back out now.
Besides, the baby's not due for three more weeks."

After much persuasion, such as only Mom can use
successfully on Dad, he agreed to go and keep the
engagement. A very reluctant Dad said, "Good-bye" to
his family and "Hello" to Chicago.

The next morning Mom came in to awaken me for
school. I took one look at her and knew that something
wasn't right.

"Is everything, okay, Mom?" I asked sleepily.

"Yes," she said, unconvincingly. "But do you mind
staying home with me today? I'm afraid I may need your
help on a few things."

I sat upright in bed. "No, Mom! You can't have
your baby today! Daddy's not here!"

But she just laughed and said, "Sheila, will you stay
with me?"

I assured her that I would, but inside I was scared.
"She can't have it today! Please, Lord, not today!"

I helped get Bob and Jeanne off to school and then
spent the rest of the day following Mom around the
house. Shortly after they left, she stopped suddenly, held
her huge tummy in her hands and took three big, slow,
painful breaths.

I was alarmed. "Mom! What's wrong?"

"Nothing. I just felt a funny twinge, that's all."

But I knew better. "That was a contraction, wasn't it?"

"Nonsense, Sheila." And off she went to make the beds.

These "funny" spells came and went all morning. Because babies weren't totally new to me, I knew to watch the clock to see how close Mom's contractions were.

Around three o'clock in the afternoon, I saw that they were only minutes apart.

"Mom! They're getting close! Don't you think you should go to the hospital?"

"Oh, I'm not ready to have this baby yet, but I do think I should go and see Dr. Zimmerman."

I called a neighbor who graciously offered to drive Mom to the doctor's office.

Meanwhile, I sat and nervously watched Carol until Bob and Jeanne came home from school. By six o'clock, I still hadn't heard from Mom, so I decided to go ahead and start dinner. "Where is she?" I worried.

I believed that the doctor had sent her to the hospital and that she hadn't had a chance to call. When the phone rang just as we had started to eat, I expected to hear, "Sheila, this is Mom. I'm at the hospital." Instead, I heard, "This is Mom. You have a new baby sister! Happy Valentine's Day!"

Carol and Gretchen, two little dolls.

I was stunned. "You had the baby already? A sister?"

Bob and Jeanne jumped up from the table and came running to the phone. Bob pulled on my arm and said, "Did you say, 'sister'?"

When I nodded, "Yes," he groaned, "Not *another* sister!"

"Now, Sheila," Mom continued, "Don't tell your father. I want to call and give him the news."

"Okay, Mom."

"Promise?"

"Yes, I promise."

"Is everything all right there?"

"Yes. We're having dinner."

"Thanks, Sheila. I knew I could count on you."

Bob, Jeanne, and I were so excited that we couldn't eat any of our dessert. I was cleaning up the kitchen when Dad called.

"Hi, Sheila!"

I gulped and thought to myself, "Dad? What's he calling here for? Didn't Mom get through to him?"

"Where's your mother?" he demanded.

"Mom?" I stalled and thought, "Obviously he doesn't know she's in the hospital. Now what do I do?"

I answered lamely, "She's not here."

"She's not there? It's dinnertime. Where in the world is she?"

"Didn't she call you, Dad?"

"No. I just got back from my lecture, and I thought I'd call and see how she is."

I realized that Dad couldn't be put off any longer. "Well, you can reach her at the hospital."

"The w-what?"

I couldn't hold it in any longer. The strain of the whole day came pouring forth as I cried, "She had the baby, Dad! It's a girl! A little valentine! H-happy Valentine's Day!"

From left to right: Bob, Sheila, Dad, Mom holding
Gretchen, Carol, and Jeanne.

"Our family is complete now," Mom assured me.

For once, Dad was speechless. Finally, he said, "A
girl—well, that's great! We wouldn't want a boy born on
Valentine's Day—would we? I'll call your mother right
away and take the first flight home. Thanks for all your
help, Sheila. I love you."

"I love you, too, Dad." It was such a relief to know that he knew and would be home soon to take care of us all.

Daddy was home that very night. And the next day he took me to see his new valentine, little Gretchen Joy.

She was beautiful! Mom looked good, too. Our family was complete, Mom assured me. "No more babies, Sheila. Your father and I have resigned ourselves to an age-old truth. When it comes to babies, all the possibility thinking in the world can't make one bit of difference."

Dad had his girls and was "outnumbered," as he often complains, "by female gadgets and female giggles." But ask any of us, his daughters whom he loves to take to dinner and show off, and we'll all concur, "Dad loves it!"

He loves the attention; he loves the service; and he loves the softness that comes with girls.

10

Rave Reviews

Bob was chasing a screaming Jeanne around the house when baby Gretchen suddenly started to cry from her playpen in the middle of the family room. I had my hands full with three-year-old Carol, who was busy clearing the table as fast as I was setting it. Meanwhile, Mom was desperately trying to salvage three pots of side dishes that had all started to boil over at once.

Into the midst of this confusion and chaos, Dad burst through the door. "Arvella! I'm home!" he cried as he strode into the kitchen. Oblivious to the din all around him, he continued, "Wait until you hear my message for tomorrow! It's terrific!"

With that, he began to preach. Mom had to duck his arms that were gesturing with as much vim and vigor as they do on any Sunday. In between screams and squeals from the younger members of the family, Dad shouted out his message enthusiastically.

Dear, patient Mother listened to every word as she tried to round up her brood for dinner. "It's a *great* message, Bob!" she said. And then she called, "Dinner! Come and get it!"

As clamorous as it was one second, the next it became just as quiet as a church as we all joined hands for prayer. This Saturday night was typical. Like most families of our size, our household was usually buzzing and humming with activity. Therefore, Mom and Dad established Saturday night and Sunday as a time for peace, meditation, and prayer.

In the same way that the Jewish Sabbath begins at nightfall on the preceding day, so in our home, Sundays really began on Saturday night. After dinner was finished, we always had our weekly circle of prayer.

"Jeanne," Dad would ask, "What are you going to pray for tonight?"

"I'm going to pray for you, Daddy," she'd reply.

Bob usually volunteered to pray for a large offering, and I offered to pray for Bob's teacher.

As we joined hands and began to pray in turn, one by one, I was often overwhelmed by my love for God, for my family, and for my church. I felt Dad's strong warm hand on my left and Gretchen's tiny helpless one on my right. One night it occurred to me, "God is powerful enough to guide strong men like my father, yet tender enough to lead tiny children like Gretchen."

Just then Dad ended the circle of prayer with a resounding "Amen" as if in positive response to my silent thoughts.

"Let's sing!" he declared.

And so we'd sing with gusto, "Surely goodness and mercy shall follow me all the days, all the days of my life!"

These Saturday night dinners were only a prelude and a preparation for the seeds that would be planted the next day. For, just as soil must be softened and fertilized before the seed is sown, so our hearts and minds were being conditioned for the message of God's love that we received every Sunday morning in church.

And in our home, the worship experience didn't stop with the church service but continued throughout the entire day. Mom and Dad feel that Sundays need to be special days, set apart from the normal tensions of everyday life. This meant that we were not allowed to play with the neighborhood children; we were not allowed to go to the store or beach; and we were not allowed to watch television.

Rather, we were encouraged to read, to write, and to work on creative projects within the home; often we went as a family for rides through the countryside. As a result, Sundays became for me a refuge, a time when my spirits were restored, and a time for contemplation when new thoughts could become deeply entrenched. It was on

The Sanctuary and Tower of Hope where
every Sunday Dad shared his messages of
hope and inspiration.

one such Sunday that God clearly showed me the steps
He wanted me to take on a matter that was very
important to me.

I was sitting on my bed with the script to the musical
Brigadoon in front of me. Tryouts for it had been
announced just the week before. When Mrs. Russ, my
high school drama teacher, called me in to talk about the
new musical, I was indeed excited.

"Sheila," she said to me. "Have you heard which
musical we've decided to do this year?"

"No, but I'm dying to know. What is it?"

"*Brigadoon.* Are you familiar with it?"

"Not really. I've heard some of the songs, but I'm
not too sure about the plot."

"Well, there's a part in it that's perfect for you. I
called you in today to tell you about it. I'm hoping you'll
audition for it."

I loved to sing and had a very good voice. I was
selected for all of the soprano solos during my senior
year in high school. In addition, I loved drama;
consequently, musicals were the perfect marriage of my
two loves.

Although it is not considered ethical for a teacher to
cast a show before auditions are held, I was terribly
flattered and excited that *I* was the one she wanted for
the role.

"It sounds wonderful! Tell me more about it."

"The play is set in the mythical town of Brigadoon

in old Scotland. There is a romantic lead, Fiona, and
there is a comedic lead, Meg. I think you would be
terrific for Meg. Here's the script. Take it home with you
and read it. Auditions are next week."

I was elated. It sounded too good to be true. I
excitedly took the script, dreaming of stardom all the
way home.

Now, here it was, Sunday afternoon. The house was
quiet; most of my family was napping. I took out the
script Mrs. Russ had given me and read it with high
hopes. Meg seemed wonderful at first—charming, witty,
and vivacious. But then I came to a scene that really
troubled me. Meg met a handsome stranger, took him
home with her, and in a light and funny scene
seduced him.

Suddenly, all my hopes were replaced with bitter
disappointment. I couldn't play a scene like that. I was a
professed Christian. Everyone knew and respected me for
my beliefs.

I closed the script, my passport to popularity at a
teeming high school, and I looked at my Bible on the
nightstand. Dad's words from his message that morning
came back to me, "What is success? It is being all that
God wants you to be!"

I thought about those words. That means that
success is not necessarily getting a good part in a
musical; but, rather, it is letting God's love shine through
me. I can't play Meg and still expect the other kids to

respect my convictions and believe in God's love.

I set the script aside, bowed my head, and prayed, "Dear Lord, I do want to be a success—for you! I want your love to shine through. I want to be what *you* want me to be. Help me do that, and show me how. Amen."

At breakfast the next morning, I announced my intentions. "Tomorrow after school, there are tryouts for the annual musical."

Dad looked up from his cereal, beaming. "That's great, Sheila! Are you going to try out for the lead? You can get it if you want it, you know!"

"Well, I thought I'd audition for Fiona. She's the romantic lead. It's risky, though, because of my height." I recalled the year before when I'd lost the lead to a shorter girl, because my six feet towered over the young men who auditioned for the male counterparts.

Bob remembered the incident, too, and quickly jumped up from his chair, craned his neck toward the ceiling, and said to an imaginary eight-foot girl, "Oh, Fiona, you must know how much I love you."

Everybody laughed. "I know. I know," I said. "There is another lead I could get, even though I am tall. Mrs. Russ practically begged me to audition for it."

"Well, why aren't you going out for that one?" Dad asked.

"Because I don't feel that as a Christian I can do the role." I recounted for them the scene and the decision that I had made regarding it.

Mom said gently, "I'm very proud of you, Sheila."

Dad concurred and added, "We'll be pulling for you as you audition for Fiona."

That afternoon I entered the auditorium. I picked up my audition card and carefully indicated that I would be auditioning for Fiona.

When my turn came, I sang my song. The singing was easy; I knew how my voice rated compared to the rest of the students, and this first audition was, as I expected, a breeze. The real trial would be at call-backs.

Call-backs, which were held the next day, were much more thorough than the first audition, and on this day I was really nervous. I sat and waited my turn, meanwhile carefully evaluating the men. I noticed that there was one boy who was tall enough to play the romantic male lead. I secretly rooted for him, knowing that my success depended on his.

I watched as Mrs. Russ indicated portions of the script that she wanted the students to read. Finally it was my turn. "Sheila, would you please come to the stage?"

I could feel my knees knock as I walked between the empty seats. As I entered the huge stage, I silently prayed, "Dear Lord, please make me a success today. Use me to let your love shine to everyone here."

Mrs. Russ handed me a script and said, "Please turn to page twenty-one and read the part of Meg."

"Meg?" I asked. I knew what she was doing. She

had already cast me in the role, even though I hadn't indicated it on the audition form. My face grew hot with hurt and anger as I felt betrayed by my drama teacher.

In front of fifty other students and a panel of teachers, I said as calmly as I could, "I'm not auditioning for Meg."

"Why not?" she demanded. "It's an excellent part!"

"It's not right for me. I can't do it. I do not feel that as a professed Christian, I can play the role of Meg."

"Sheila, I asked you to read the part. Now are you going to read or not?"

I could see that the only way to convince her that I was not right for the role, would be to read it for her. So, I read—as slowly and as monotonously as I could. It sounded terrible! Mrs. Russ knew my capabilities as an actress, and she could see that I was deliberately reading the worst I could. Since the other teachers had witnessed my flunky performance, she would be forced to give the role to another girl.

I gave the script back to Mrs. Russ. She was stunned to say the least. But I walked out of that auditorium with my head held high.

I no sooner got out of the room, however, than I began to feel the tremendous disappointment well within me. I ran to the parking lot where I knew Dad was waiting for me.

I threw open the car door and flung myself into his arms. "Oh Dad! Oh Dad! I didn't get the part of Fiona!

She never even intended for me to read it. She was dead set that I do Meg."

There in the comfort of my father's arms, I spilled out the entire scene. Finally, I looked up at him, still crying, and asked, "Why did she do that to me in front of all those kids?"

Dad, eyes shimmering with a shared hurt but gleaming with pride, said, "Sheila, don't you see? God allowed it to happen today so that you could make a statement of your faith in front of all those students. I am so proud of you! God chose you to play an exceptional part today! He chose you out of all the other students to share in a loving way that Jesus is Lord of your life."

He looked me squarely in the eye and continued, "This afternoon, you were a smashing success! You get rave reviews from God and from me!"

"R-really, Dad?"

"Really, Sheila! In fact, I am more proud of you today, than if you had opened on Broadway."

Dad helped me see the all-important role that God had chosen for me that year at high school. And it was with great delight that I accepted the request from my choir director to sing the "O Holy Night" solo for the entire student body at the annual Christmas assembly.

As I stood on my special platform, with its stained glass backdrop flanked by the hundred-voice choir and entire orchestra, I sang with all my heart to every one of my friends and fellow students:

O Holy Night, the stars are brightly shining.
It is the night of the dear Savior's birth.
Long lay the world in sin and error pining
Till He appeared and the soul felt its worth.
A thrill of hope, the weary world rejoices,
For yonder breaks a new and glorious morn.

Fall on your knees,
O hear the angel voices,
O night divine,
O night when Christ was born.
O night divine,
O night, O night divine!

11

Going and Growing

I bounced determinedly on the stubborn suitcase as
Mom quickly snapped it shut. "Got it!" she cried
triumphantly. "That should do it. Now, I'll get Dad to
carry this out to the car. Meanwhile, you check and
make sure that you haven't forgotten anything."

She rustled out in her robe as I began to look
aimlessly around my room. I tried vainly to remember all
the things I would need, but all I could think of was my
family and how much I'd miss them. All of a sudden I
felt a knot begin to grow in my chest.

"I'd better get out of here before it's too late," I
thought, as I quickly grabbed my purse and coat and
scurried out to the kitchen where Mom was pouring
coffee.

"Do you have everything?" she asked.

"Yes," I answered.

Mom continued to bustle about in her usual practical manner, her eyes purposely avoiding mine.

Just then, Dad called, "It's time to go, Sheila!"

Mom followed me to the door. She had opted to stay home. "It's easier to say good-bye, here," she explained.

The light from the porch lamp was needed in the early morning hour, and Mom looked soft and warm standing in its glow.

"I can't let myself think how much I'll miss her," I thought as she hugged me gently. Her cheek was moist as it brushed mine.

"Good-bye, Sheila," she said, her voice catching slightly. "Write often, and call just as soon as you get there."

The knot had been growing all morning. Now it was a hard, aching lump. I turned quickly and ran to the car.

As I slid into the front seat, I felt with all my being that I didn't want to go. Although I had been excited about leaving for college the night before, now I was only scared and homesick.

Dad started the car, and we began our last father-daughter ride to school. The sun was just beginning to rise behind us as we headed for Los Angeles airport; and we hadn't been on the freeway very long, when we came up over the familiar rise. There, still illuminated with its night lights, was the cross on the Tower of Hope. How many times I had looked at that cross and found strength and peace and comfort. It would be a long time before I would see it or my family again.

I looked over at Dad and realized how terribly I'd miss him. Grasping desperately for something to hold me together, I latched onto a poem he had taught me on a previous ride to school.

"Dad . . ." I started hesitantly, "Do you remember the poem you taught me? The one that goes:

> Grieve not for me who am about to start
> A new adventure.
> Eager I stand and ready to depart,
> Me and my reckless, pioneering heart.

"That's terrific, Sheila! That's the attitude!"

Reciting the poem really helped. It made me feel adventuresome and brave, and I almost began to look forward to my journey.

We checked my baggage and soon my flight was called. I felt Dad's big, strong arms envelop me in a bear hug.

"Good-bye, Sheila. I'll miss you."

The knot had crept into my throat again. It ached as I said, "Bye, Dad. I'll miss you, too."

With that, I turned and walked as fast as I could down the long gangway, away from him. Suddenly, I wheeled around for one last wave.

But Dad didn't see me. He was already on his way back to the car. Yet, just as I was about to lose sight of him, I saw him brusquely wipe his eyes.

I couldn't hold it any longer. The knot burst, and with it came a flood of tears. The stewardess thoughtfully ignored my red eyes, for I'm sure she was touched by the sight of a sensitive young college girl who was failing miserably at being adventuresome and sophisticated.

Hope College is set in southwestern Michigan, nestled against Lake Michigan. For a California-bred girl, it was breathtakingly beautiful. The tall, old trees arch gracefully across the walkways, and the ivy clings to the walls of the early Dutch buildings. The college is steeped in tradition. I loved it immediately!

When I arrived, I found that the college had mistakenly enrolled more students than the dormitories could accommodate. This required them to purchase some old homes adjacent to the campus and assign freshmen to them. I was one of those freshmen.

After I had seen the lovely campus, I was brought to my residence. What a sore disappointment! Beck Cottage was decrepit, and my room a shambles. I used every ounce of possibility thinking I could muster as I unpacked my things. I tore through my bags, found the plaque I had brought, and hung it immediately. It said, "Bloom where you are planted."

"Okay," I said to myself, "You're here for a whole year. You can either look for the good and enjoy it, or be miserable."

Because Beck was small, there were only eight of us living there; and because we were removed from the other dorms, where we could meet a lot of different girls, we stuck together and became very close.

To say that my first year at Hope was "eventful"

would be an understatement. I don't think I've ever grown or learned more than I did my freshman year.

One morning I was merely walking back to Beck from the dining room, where I had just had breakfast. No sooner did I turn the corner that lead to my street than I saw three long fire engines parked in front of three houses. One of them was ours.

"Oh, no! Which house is on fire?" I thought.

But then I saw one truck pull away, then another. That left only one—the one parked smack dab in front of Beck. I quickened my steps and began to run. I could hardly believe my eyes! I could see that they were carrying articles out of the house, and the articles belonged to me!

The fire chief, seeing me approach, demanded, "Do you live here?"

"Yes, I do. Those are my things," I said as I pointed to some charred, soggy books lying in the grass.

I suddenly found myself not only the victim of a fire, but also a victim of an angry fire chief, as he proceeded to give me a thorough lecture on fire safety and overloading the electrical systems of old homes.

"Yeah," I said to myself, "But you should be giving this lecture to the other girls. I've told them hundreds of times not to use those multiple plugs in the sockets. So who's stuff gets burned? Mine!"

Actually, very little was damaged, other than my ego. Incidents like this became the norm for us, and we soon found ourselves with the unflattering nickname of "Beck's Bruisers."

Nevertheless, I had fallen in love with Hope College. I loved the fall, with its brilliantly colored leaves and the crisp air that heralded the coming of winter. And I'll never forget our first snowfall.

I had had trouble finding boots that summer in sunny California. So Mom decided to wait and get me a pair when I came home for Christmas vacation. Unfortunately, the snow didn't wait. One afternoon while I was studying by my window, I happened to look outside. There were big, lacy flakes floating down and settling on the windowsill and everywhere else. In no time at all, my world became a white wonder. I quickly abandoned my studies and ran out to play in it, tennis shoes and all.

As Christmas vacation approached, I could hardly believe that I had been away from home four months. What I had thought would pass like four years, had flown by. But as vacation drew near, so did final exams.

One night while studying for my philosophy exam with Gail, a fellow "Beck Bruiser," she interrupted my reading with, "Sheila, do you really believe in God? I mean, you're always reading your Bible and stuff, and I know your father's a minister, but do you *really* believe in God? Do you feel Him deep down inside?"

I immediately put down my book and looked up with surprise. Of all the girls who lived at Beck Cottage, she was the one who had been the hardest to get close to. She made no pretenses about where she stood on such matters as religion, dating, drugs, etc. There was always a tough shell surrounding her, though there were times when I had the feeling that she was daring someone to crack it.

I looked up into her troubled eyes and said, "Yes, Gail. I do believe in God. And I do feel Him deep down inside. I feel my love for Him and His love for me."

"I wish I could! I really wish I could!" And off she ran to her room, never giving me a chance to reply.

From that moment on, I looked for opportunities to continue my conversation with her. But, she made it perfectly clear that she didn't want to discuss it any further.

Finally, it was time for Christmas vacation. That was the most joyous flight of my life! When my plane descended over the lights of Los Angeles, I knew I was home. What a fantastic sight it was to see Mom and Dad running to me, with open arms, and to feel them hugging me again!

Vacation was heavenly! But it was all over too soon. It seemed that I had hardly gotten home and had barely unpacked and unwrapped Christmas gifts, than it was time to head back. This time, however, I didn't dread the return trip, for I knew I had friends waiting for me, and I knew that it wouldn't be long before I'd be home for summer vacation.

But January and February are long months in Holland, Michigan. The snow is no longer fresh. The sidewalks are slippery and treacherous, especially if you're late for class. The wind that whips off that lake cuts through the warmest of coats, and the sun is shielded by a steel-gray sky for weeks on end.

The only bright spot in this whole time was a phone call I got from home. "Sheila! Guess what!" It was Dad. He was as exuberant as ever. "I'm going to be out in Holland next week for some meetings. Do you think you could spare some time to spend with me?"

"Do I? That's fantastic!" I replied. I longingly counted the hours until the afternoon that Dad was scheduled to arrive. I heard the snow crunch beneath the car just as soon as it pulled into the driveway. From my window I could see Dad as he emerged from the rental car. His strong silhouette, wrapped in a dark overcoat, looked so warm and welcome against the cold, bleak background.

I flew down the stairs and into his arms. "Dad! Dad! It's so good to see you!"

He laughed and gave me his usual bear hug. "Would you like to go get some coffee with me?"

"I'd love it!"

Over coffee, we caught up on news, and Dad explained the nature of his meetings. They had something to do with the college, so he would be on the campus for the majority of his visit.

"Sheila," he suggested, "You know, I'm going to be in meetings for a couple of hours every afternoon, so feel free to use my hotel room as a quiet place to study. It's perfect for catching up on all those classes you might be behind in," he added with a twinkle.

It sounded good, and as I *was* behind, I took him up on it. It was quiet, and I got a lot done. After studying for about three hours, I decided that I should start the walk back to Beck to get ready for dinner. Dad was taking me out before his plane left, and I wanted to look especially nice.

I had no sooner turned the corner leading to our cottage, than I saw Janet and Dana, two of the girls who lived in Beck with me. Strangely, they were carrying Gail's coat.

When Janet saw me she cried out, "Oh, Sheila! It's so terrible!"

"What is it, Janet? What's happened?" The anguish in their faces scared me.

"It's Gail! We don't know if she's going to make it or not!"

"What do you mean?"

"She took a whole lot of pills, and she's in the hospital. She's in a coma."

I was stunned. I couldn't believe it. "Oh, Gail!" I thought. "You've got to make it! I still have so much to tell you about Jesus and His love for you."

Totally shaken, I dropped my books off at the cottage and then ran immediately to find Dad. I stood outside the room where he told me he'd be and prayed frantically for the meeting to end. I couldn't hold on much longer. "What if we lose her?" I thought over and over.

Finally, a student aide came out of the meeting room.

"Excuse me," I said, "But do you know if the meeting in there is almost over?"

"Your father is Dr. Schuller, isn't he?"

"Yes."

"Well, I'll be glad to tell him that you need to
see him."

"Oh, thank you! I'd really appreciate it!"

Seconds later Dad emerged and I buried myself in
his arms. After I had relayed the whole tragic incident,
he said, "Let's get out of here."

In silence, he led me out of the building and walked
with me arm-in-arm along the icy sidewalks. After a long
time he said gently, "Sheila, trouble never leaves you
where it finds you. It will either leave you a better
person, or a bitter person. You can choose which it
will be."

His words melted through the icy knot in the pit of
my heart and warmed me thoroughly. As we continued
our walk, it was as though we left grief behind and
gained more and more strength with each step we took.

Dad tightened his arm around me and said, "Sheila,
do you remember the phrase, 'In love's service, only
broken hearts will do'?"

"Yes."

"Well, you are experiencing today the real hurt and
agony that comes with a broken heart. Only people who
have experienced what you are feeling now can be
compassionate enough to help others. Let God take your
hurt and use it to make you a better person, a special
person—one who's fit for love's service."

I resolved then and there not to let Gail's life go to
waste. No matter what the outcome, whether she lived or
died, I promised Dad that I would let God use the hurt.

As we reached Beck, I turned to Dad and hugged

him as tightly as I could. "Thanks, Dad. Thanks so much for being here."

As I said good-bye to him, it struck me how gracious God had been in placing him there when I needed him. Buoyed by the strength I received from my father and my Lord, I went to join the other grieving girls within the cottage.

Gail's life hung in the balance for three more days. One evening, we came home from dinner to hear the news that she was gone.

"It was for the best," the doctors said. "She would have been a vegetable all her life. The thirty Darvon that she took were immediately absorbed into her blood stream. They relaxed her heart until it stopped beating, and the lack of oxygen to her brain left irrevocable damage."

No one knows just why she did it. I do know that she regretted it, for she fearfully asked her roommate when she got to the hospital, "I'm not going to die, am I?"

Gail's life was short. It was tragic. But it had a tremendous impact on mine. Since then, I have seen many "Gails." Most of them have not physically taken their lives, but many are dying inside. Today, when I see a girl who's confused, lost, and hurting, I remember Gail; and I remember Dad's words, "In love's service, only broken hearts will do." And then I know that *I* will do. I can sign up for love's service, for I know how fatal a broken heart can be.

12

My Gem, Jim

I lay in the top bed of the bunk that I shared with my roommate, Cindy. I could just see part of her in our tiny bathroom as she rolled up her long, thick hair. I couldn't believe that this was our last night at Hope. The years had flown. Tomorrow we'd don our caps and gowns and parade to "Pomp and Circumstance" as proud graduates. The long, grueling nights of studying, attending sorority parties, spying on friends as they whispered fond farewells to boyfriends, sharing intimate secrets, fears, and dreams—all of these would be gone forever.

I felt a tear trickle slowly out of the corner of my eye. "How ironic!" I scolded myself. "Four years ago, you cried because you had to leave home to come here. Now those years are over, and you can't bear to see them end."

I quickly turned my face to the wall so Cindy couldn't see me crying. But it didn't work. The next minute I felt her hand on my shoulder. "Sheila?" she asked, her own voice a little shaky, "You're not crying, are you?"

I turned to her and let the tears flow freely. "Yes! I am!"

She laughed and hugged me, and we cried together. I was not the only senior to cry herself to sleep that night. Our bunk beds rocked with silent tears deep into the night.

Mom and Dad couldn't believe it when they picked me up for breakfast the next morning. All I did was cry. "Aren't you glad to see us?" Dad teased.

Mom just chuckled, "I hadn't planned on flying all the way to Michigan just to dry your tears!"

Class of '73.

Despite their teasing, I knew they understood. "I'm sorry," I said. "I'll try to be brave."

"Come on," Dad said, "Isn't it about time we got ready to receive our degrees?"

He was beaming. He was going to receive a degree at the same service in which I'd be receiving my B.A., for Dad had been chosen to receive an honorary doctorate from Hope, his Alma Mater. He had dreamed of this day for a long time. I was very proud of Dad as he was bestowed the highest honor a college can give.

Back in California I found that I was terribly lost and lonely. Cindy was in Illinois, and the rest of my friends were scattered throughout the Midwest or along the Eastern coastline.

Mom and Dad were wise enough to see that what I needed was a project. One day, as Mom brought me along to drop Jeanne off at a junior-high picnic, she slyly observed, "They certainly look like they'd be a lot of fun."

I had to agree with her, for I found myself envying these carefree young people. It seemed as though they all had more friends than they knew what to do with.

"You know, Sheila, the junior-high department is looking for leaders. Do you think you'd like to help out?"

It sounded wonderful! The other leaders, who were college age like me, looked as though they were having as much fun as the zany kids. Before I knew what hit me, I became thoroughly involved with the junior-high youngsters.

The involvement grew over the years, until I found myself giving leadership not only to junior-high students, but senior-high, and college students as well. During four happy years I threw my entire life into youth ministries—counseling students about their problems, directing and producing musicals for the creative, painting sets with the artistic, planning fashion shows for the seamstresses, and attempting softball, volleyball, and even football with the athletes.

It was the most thrilling and fulfilling life I could imagine. There was only one small void. After each long, delightful day with the young people was over, I dreaded going home to my lonely apartment. Consequently, I filled every waking hour I could to keep from having to face my loneliness. When I didn't have a Bible study or a rehearsal, I'd go and visit Mom and Dad.

That only made matters worse, though, for Mom and Dad were a living example of the fulfillment that comes with marriage. I longed and ached for the day when I could have such a marriage, when I could have a husband, when I could have a home of my own.

One night, dear, sensitive Dad tried to help. Knowing that something was bothering me, he asked, "What's wrong, Sheila? You seem so unhappy tonight."

"Oh, Dad, it's so hard sometimes to be single. I really love working with young people, but I don't want to do that my entire life."

"What do you want?"

It has always been so easy to be open with Dad. All

I have to do is look into his soft, understanding eyes,
and everything tumbles out.

"I want to get married!" I blurted out. "I want to
have a husband who'll treat me as beautifully as you
treat Mom. I want a man who will value me as a
priceless teacup." All the pent-up hurt, fears, and
loneliness came pouring forth in a stream of sobs
and tears.

Dad wrapped his loving arms around me and let me
cry and cry and cry. Finally, he cupped my chin in his
hands and brought my eyes to meet his. They were
glistening, sharing my hurt.

"Sheila, that is a noble dream. Every woman should
have a person who will treat her as a precious gem. I'm
going to pray that God will send you a man like that.
Meanwhile, you pray that God will make you into the
woman that this wonderful man will need. Then, when
the time is right and when both of you are right, God
will answer our prayer."

Never in my wildest dreams did I imagine that God
would answer my prayer in the way that He did, for He
started answering my prayer immediately, right before
my unsuspecting eyes.

I had met a certain young man only briefly at church.
He was a free-lance artist that I had contacted for a
youth brochure. He was probably the furthest from my
"ideal man" that I could ever hope to meet.

Actually, I *heard* him coming before I saw him. His
sporty, red Porsche came roaring through the parking
lot. Some of the senior-high boys who were in my office

at the time whistled, "Man! That's some car! Is *that* the artist you're meeting today, Sheila?"

I was very curious. I ran to the window overlooking the parking lot and there, striding toward the building, was the most "arty" looking young man I'd ever seen. To a sheltered preacher's kid, this tall, lanky man with a ponytail and a voluminous walrus mustache looked like a hippy. In retrospect, I'm sure I must have appeared like a missionary to him.

Our meeting was very uneventful. Jim did the artwork that I requested, and that was that.

I never gave him another thought until one day, a few months later, when I arrived at the youth center. There was a great deal of hubbub in the office next to mine, so I peeked in to see what was going on. There was this same artist, Jim Coleman, moving boxes aside to make room for the drafting table that was propped against the wall.

"Jim?" I asked, curious as to what he was doing there at that time of day and wondering what all those boxes meant.

"Oh, hi, Sheila!" he said jovially.

"W-What are you doing?" I inquired.

"You haven't heard? I'm going to be your new neighbor! The church has hired me on as a full-time artist."

"Really?" I gulped. He seemed strange to me, but he also seemed nice. "Well, welcome neighbor!"

And so began a warm and wonderful friendship. Because Jim was not "my type," I found it easy to be relaxed with him. With the absence of romantic overtones, our friendship was free to develop as we worked side by side over the years.

Gradually, during the next three years, Jim began to change. When he first came to work at the church, he was a professed "non-Christian." He came from a wonderful home where he was raised to go to church, yet he had never come to a point where he had given his life over to Jesus as his personal friend and Savior.

I couldn't believe that such a talented and gentle man could work day by day with some of the most beautiful Christians and still not be a Christian. Many of us prayed for him. We had all grown to love him and wanted more than anything for him to find the love of God that only comes in an intimate relationship with His Son, Jesus.

One day, I walked into Jim's office and found him reading a Bible. I was shocked! Because I didn't know why he was reading it, and because I didn't want to be pushy, I ignored it, suppressed my excitement, and nonchalantly said, "Hi, Jim! I'm not interrupting anything, am I?"

He smiled and said, "No, I'm not busy."

I desperately tried to read his eyes. "Were they different from the last time I saw him?" I wondered.

But Jim interrupted my thoughts, "Is there something I can do for you?"

"Oh! Well . . . " I had totally forgotten what I had

come in to see him about. To my relief, my memory began functioning again. "I was wondering, have you finished the layout for the girls' brochure?"

He had, and after I quickly read it and gave it my approval, I dashed excitedly to the office of Gary DeVaul, the College Director. Gary, too, had befriended Jim.

"Gary! Guess what! I just saw *Jim Coleman* reading a *Bible*! Do you think . . .?"

Gary didn't even let me finish my question as he dashed out to Jim's office. There Jim shared with him, "Gary, I'm beginning to consider the possibility that all the writers of the Bible are indeed telling the truth about Jesus—that it's not something they just made up. They actually lived with him, walked with him, talked with him, and saw him heal people as no one else had ever done!"

I was thrilled when I learned how the ministry was transforming another life as it had thousands of others. And I thanked God for answering our prayers as I saw Jim blossom and grow into a beautiful man of God.

Meanwhile, Jim and I continued to be friends, never dreaming that God was bringing us closer and closer to the culmination of His plan for us.

Although we had been friends for almost four years now, I had never felt the least romantic feeling for him.

One day I was sitting at my desk working on a project when Jim happened to walk by, as he had done hundreds of times. This time, however, it was different. When he strode past my desk, my heart did a complete flip-flop.

"He surely is handsome," I thought. "And he's so tall, and his eyes are the deepest blue I've ever seen."

To my surprise I realized that I was in love. I fell fast and I fell hard. Then I started to worry. "What if Jim realizes how I feel about him? Will he still want to be my friend?" I became very nervous whenever I had to talk to him, and I prayed and prayed that God would help me to be calm and to be myself.

One day I found this little note on my desk. I recognized Jim's handwriting. I could hardly open it because of the excitement that I felt, and then I read the words I had dreamed and longed to hear. "Sheila, you look beautiful again today. I want you to know how much I have enjoyed working with you."

"Oh, what does he mean?" I wondered. "Does he mean that I'm beautiful to look at? Or does he mean 'beautiful'—the way a friend is beautiful—inside." I was confused, but definitely encouraged.

My heart sang that day; I couldn't, for the life of me, keep my mind on my work. Finally, thoroughly frustrated with sitting behind my desk, I made up an excuse to walk around the church grounds.

As I wandered among the beautiful shrubs and flowers, I looked up at the gorgeous blue sky with its drifting, billowing clouds. My eyes, dancing with hope, settled at last on the cross, looming on top of the Tower of Hope. "Lord Jesus," I prayed, "I know that I have foolishly asked You for certain men before, and I was foolish in asking. But I'm going to ask again. If it be

Your will, I'd like for this love I feel for Jim to
work out."

Two days later I heard God's resounding, "Yes!"
when Jim asked me out. As I found out later, God had
planted the same romantic stirrings in Jim at the time He
planted them in me. After five wonderful months of
dating, Jim asked me to be his bride.

Dad had been suspicious that Jim would propose while
he and Mom were gone on summer vacation; and I was
instructed when I dropped them off at the airport to call
them, "No matter where we are, to let us know of any
good news."

It was with delight that I called the overseas
operator and heard the phone ring in their Hong Kong
hotel room.

"Hello?" Dad didn't sound as if he were halfway
around the world.

"Hi, Dad! This is Sheila!" I paused dramatically.
"How does a February wedding sound?"

"Oh, Sheila! Did he? Oh, I'm *so* glad! Why, if I
could search the whole world over, I could not find as
wonderful a man for you as your Jim."

Mom got on the phone then and said, "Sheila! What
wonderful news! Plan an engagement party for when we
get home. Check Dad's calendar. Invite whomever you
wish. It will be a joyous event!"

Then we called Jeanne at Wheaton College where
she was preparing for a summer quarter in Jerusalem.

"Jeanne?" I asked when she sleepily answered the phone, "Would you like to be my maid of honor?"

"Oh, Sheila!" she screamed and screamed some more, "I'm so happy!" I have never heard anyone as excited about being in a wedding as was Jeanne.

Bob and his wife, Linda, were in the Holy Land, and there was no phone number where they could be reached. But Carol and Gretchen, staying at Uncle Henry's farm, were close enough to call.

Aunt Alberta answered the phone and ran to get the girls from the barn. Soon I heard little feet scurrying to the phone and Carol asking breathlessly, "Sheila?"

"Yes."

"How are you?"

"I'm fine, Carol. I have some good news for you and Gretchen. Jim has asked me to marry him!"

"No kidding? You accepted, of course, didn't you?"

"Oh, yes!"

"Oh, Sheila! I'm so glad! I love Jim! When will you get your ring?"

"I have it already. Jim gave it to me when he proposed."

"How romantic! I can hardly wait to see it."

"Well, I can't wait to show it to you! But it won't be long. I'll be picking you and Gretchen up at the airport in only two weeks. Be good, Carol. I love you!"

"I love you, too!"

13

Change of Plans

The balmy, summer night air sailed through the car as Jim and I drove home after a long, delightful day at his parents' house. "We are so lucky," I thought, "to have so many people so happy about our engagement."

As we sped along the freeway, the oncoming lights of the cars reminded me of a giant diamond bracelet weaving its way through the canyon. "Diamonds . . ." my thoughts continued, "Tomorrow I pick up Carol and Gretchen at the airport. I can hardly wait to show them my ring. They'll be so excited!"

As if he had heard my thoughts, Jim asked, "Are you looking forward to seeing Carol and Gretchen tomorrow?"

"Yes! I've really missed them. It's been over a month, you know."

"And when do your parents get home?"

"In another week. I'm going to stay with the girls over the weekend and then bring them to church Monday morning where they'll meet the bus for camp. Carol's helping out as a junior counselor this year."

"Really? It's hard to believe that Carol's grown as much as she has this year," Jim commented. "Just before the girls left, it struck me how beautiful Carol has become. She has really blossomed into a charming young woman."

I had noticed it, too. Carol had changed overnight from a gangly young girl into a beautiful young lady.

Just then the warm night air, combined with the fatigue of a long day, lulled me to sleep. Jim, seeing my nod and hearing my silence, suggested, "Sheila, you have to get up early tomorrow. Why don't you just sleep the rest of the way home. It's late and you need your rest."

Jim didn't know how true his words were, for that last little nap was all the sleep I was to get for two more days.

He gently awoke me when we reached my apartment and, in his usual gentlemanly way, walked me to my door.

Hanging there was a note which said, "Sheila, there's been an accident. Carol may have broken her leg. Call Mike Nason."

"Now what!" I laughed. "What has Carol gotten herself into this time? And if she has broken her leg what will that do to their flight home in the morning?"

Jim came in with me as I dialed Mike's number.
Mike is the producer of the "Hour of Power" and a dear
friend of the family. He and his wife, Donna, have a
beautiful daughter, Tara, who was in an accident a few
years ago. She may never be able to walk again, but God
is very real in both Tara's and her parents' lives.

Donna answered the phone. "Is Mike there?" I
asked.

"He's on the other line, Sheila. He's talking to your
father in Korea."

"Is it that serious?"

"Oh, yes, Sheila. It's very serious." Donna's voice
was tight, and it sent a chill through me. "She's been in a
motorcycle accident. It looks like she might lose
her leg."

The words hit me cold and hard. I felt as though the
breath had been knocked out of me, and the emotional
pain that shot through me caused me to double over
in half.

Jim looked at me horrified. "Sheila! What in the
world is wrong?"

"I-It's Carol. S-She's been in a motorcycle accident.
She might l-lose her l-leg." My whole being felt as
though it were being torn apart. Jim quickly took me
and held me tightly.

"Oh, Jim! What are we going to do?"

"Well, first of all, we don't know for sure if she'll
lose her leg or not. So, we'll wait for Uncle Henry's call,
and meanwhile we'll pray."

As he prayed I felt a powerful sense of strength surge within me. I was buoyed by the all-loving arms of my Heavenly Father.

I recalled words Dad had taught us, "Possibility thinking, which is just another word for faith, will carry you through any crisis you may encounter. Use it to plug into God's power. Use it to bring God's plan into focus. Use it to tap into the God-given ability to see good in any situation, to see the silver lining behind the cloud, the rainbow in the midst of rain, the possible in the impossible."

I felt momentarily strengthened, and then the phone rang. It was Uncle Henry. "Sheila," his voice was shaky, "I've just finished talking to the doctor. He said that there's no way they can save Carol's leg. She's in surgery now. They are going to amputate."

"Oh, no!" I paused a moment and then asked, "Does Dad know?"

"I haven't called him, yet. Do you want to?"

"I don't mind calling him."

With Jim's strong arm around me, I dialed the overseas operator for the second time in just two short weeks. How different this call was from the last one.

"H-hello?" Dad answered. His voice was as drawn and lifeless as I've ever heard it.

"Dad? This is Sheila. How are you doing?"

"Well, we've had bad news, you know," and then his voice broke as he began to cry.

"She'll be all right, Dad. She's in God's care."

"We're waiting to hear if they'll be able to save her leg or not. Your Mother and I feel confident that the doctor will be able to save it. We've been praying and praying for that."

"Dad," I interrupted, then gulped and with a prayer continued, "Dad—her leg is severely crushed. There's no way the doctors can repair the damage. They're taking it now."

"Oh, no!" and then he began to sob softly, a continent away.

Then Mom took the phone. "What is it, Sheila?"

"They can't save the leg, Mom. They're doing the amputation now."

At first there was silence, and then Mom said very slowly, carefully forming each word through her tears, "ALL THINGS WORK TOGETHER FOR GOOD TO THEM THAT LOVE GOD."

Although I had heard this Bible verse thousands of times in my life, and although it had been a keystone phrase in Mom and Dad's ministry since the very beginning, it was as though I was hearing the words for the first time. Never have I heard them said with such force and such conviction.

"Yes, Mom, I believe it, too. When will you and Dad be able to get there?"

"It's a fourteen-hour flight. That is *if* we can get a flight."

"Carol will be out of surgery in about four hours. I'll be glad to take the first flight I can, so that I can be there with her when she comes out of anesthesia."

"Oh, Sheila, that would be great. I can't think of anyone who could better take our place there than you."

"She's in God's care, Mom. No one loves her more than He does."

"Yes, that's right," her voice cracked.

"Hurry home, Mom."

The strength I had felt upholding me during the phone call left as soon as I hung up. "Oh, Jim!" I cried. "How can I go and face Carol by myself?" I looked up into his compassionate eyes and suddenly pleaded, "Jim, will you go with me? I can be strong for Carol if I have you to lean on."

He graciously conceded and then proceeded to make our reservations. He stayed with me throughout the night, helping me pack, making me coffee, holding my hand, and praying constantly with me.

That night is one I'll never forget. It was filled with God's incredible strength, and yet there were terrible moments of grief as God brought before me the issues in stark reality.

First, I dealt with visions of Carol. I saw her first as an infant, home from the hospital. She had *two* legs. Now, she had only one. Then I saw her as a toddler, teetering on her unstable legs. But, at least there were *two*. Now, there was only one. Then I saw her as she looked on her thirteenth birthday, dressed so smartly in her plaid, pleated skirt. With it, she wore her first pair of nylons which softly shaded her shapely legs—*both* legs. Now there was only one.

The thought was grisly. I wept openly and bitterly. But through my tears I heard God say, "A leg is only flesh and bones. It is from dust; to dust it will return. But the spirit lives on forever. I will make Carol's spirit more beautiful than it ever could have been had she gone through life with *two* legs. She has *Me*—and that she will never lose!"

As Jim and I drove to the airport in the wee hours of that day, we were still stunned and shaky but filled with God's power and our love for each other. The ride was far different from that which had been originally planned. I was to have picked up Carol and Gretchen, both whole and healthy. Instead, we were boarding a plane, having no idea what we'd find at the end of our flight.

When we landed at Sioux City, we were greeted by Uncle Henry. His weary eyes, filled with tears, matched his weak, hoarse voice.

"How is she?" I anxiously asked.

"We came close to losing her."

"Losing her? What do you mean?"

"The doctors say that it is a miracle that she's alive."

With difficulty, Uncle Henry told us about the accident. He shared with us how our cousin Mark had taken Carol for a motorcycle ride on her last night in Iowa. It had been at Carol's request. She had worn a helmet after Mark had insisted.

As they drove down the country road, the car in

front of them suddenly screeched to a halt. Mark, seeing that he was unable to avoid crashing into the rear end of the car, swerved to the left, where out of the night came another car, swiping the full left-hand side of the bike and their bodies.

"Carol's leg carried the brunt of the impact. She lay in the ditch and lost almost all of her blood before the ambulance could get there," Uncle Henry explained.

"Then, when they got her to the hospital, she almost bled to death in surgery. It was either her leg or her life."

I had had no idea Carol had come so close to death. As I realized how fortunate we were to have her alive, I suddenly felt ashamed of grieving so for her leg. If only I had seen earlier that I must look not at what was lost, but at what was *saved*—her *life*!

No sooner had Jim and I entered the Sioux City hospital, than Gretchen came running up to us, throwing her arms around my waist. As I held Gretchen as tightly as I could, my hand brushed her cheek. It was like ice.

"Gretchen!" I asked, "Why is your face so cold?"

"Well, they let me see Carol a few minutes ago. There were all these tubes running into her and bottles of blood . . . and . . . well, I fainted."

Poor Gretchen! What a sight that must have been for an eleven-year-old.

"Is she awake, Gretchen? Can I go see her?"

"I think so."

Jim and I walked apprehensively toward the

intensive care unit. Just outside Carol's room, he took me and held both of my hands in his. "Are you ready for this?"

"Yes." I mustered up all the courage I had within me; and with a prayer in my heart, we entered Carol's room.

"Hi, Sheila! Hi, Jim!" Carol said enthusiastically. "Oh, Sheila! Let me see your ring!"

My fears quickly flew, and my eyes barely saw her bruised, swollen face or the cloth-draped stump suspended by the traction wires. All I saw was a beautiful, radiant girl. It was clear that Someone had gotten to Carol's bedside long before Jim and I.

God had been with Carol every minute she lay in the ditch, bleeding and in excruciating pain, every minute as she waited close to half an hour for an ambulance; and He had been with the surgeon, guiding his incisions and decisions. He had been with Carol when she regained consciousness, only to discover that she was now minus part of a major limb.

Carol's high spirits were quickly dampened by the pain and nightmares that neither morphine nor sleeping pills could erase.

When Jeanne flew in from Wheaton, she and Jim and I took turns sitting with Carol, wiping her fevered brow, stroking her cheek, and holding her hand. As she drifted in and out of a sleep that lasted only minutes at a time, she would always jerk awake, her eyes wide with terror.

"It's okay, Carol," we'd reassure her. "You're all

right. You're safe here in bed, and we're right here."

Then she'd drift back to sleep, only to jump awake minutes later.

This went on throughout the day and throughout the night.

Finally, we received word that Mom and Dad had been able to get a flight out of Korea and would be landing in Sioux City at five the next morning. Jeanne volunteered to stay with Carol while Jim and I went to meet them.

The wind whipped around our tired bodies as we waited for their flight out on the runway of the tiny airport. Soon, we saw the lights of the plane as it approached through the early morning darkness. As it landed, and Mom and Dad stepped down from the plane, I was suddenly overcome with a mixture of relief and grief. I was so glad that they were finally there to relieve me of my burden.

I ran across the empty expanse to Dad's arms, "Oh, Dad, you can be so proud of Carol! She's doing fantastically!"

I looked up into his tense, teary eyes and saw a flicker of hope and gratitude. "Really?"

"Yes, I know you'll feel so much better just seeing her."

With that, we dashed to the hospital. Mom and Dad, though they had been without sleep for over thirty hours, seemed concerned, yet at peace. With long, fast strides down the corridor, we hurried to be at Carol's side.

There was that moment of hesitation for Mom and Dad as there had been for Jim and me just before we had entered Carol's room for the first time. I watched Dad carefully as he struggled to hold onto all the power he had within himself and from His Lord.

But as he and Mom went in, they, too, were greeted by Carol with a cheery, "Mom! Dad! I'm so glad you're here."

Dad, blinking back the tears that stung his eyes, said bravely, "Carol, I'm glad we're here, too."

But Carol enthusiastically interrupted him, "I think I know why God allowed this to happen to me."

"Oh?" questioned Dad.

"I think God wants to use me to help other people who have been hurt."

Carol's spirit made all of us so very proud and so very grateful for the positive Christian faith with which we had been so graciously endowed.

We received calls from friends and loved ones across the country, including Oral Roberts, who had a beautiful prayer with Dad on the phone.

Although Carol's spirits were in top condition, physically she was still critical. The doctor had amputated just below the left knee, though her injury extended well into her thigh. Because her severed, torn leg had been dragged through the dirt, infection was a vital concern.

The next day, as Carol's fever continued to soar, the

doctor approached Dad. "Carol needs more surgery," he
advised, "and I would like to have your permission to
amputate the knee if I feel it's necessary."

This hit Dad hard. He had originally heard that
Carol would probably lose her foot; then, he was told
she would lose almost half a leg. "At least she still has
her knee," we had reasoned.

But now, even that was threatened.

Dad called Cory Servaas, a dear friend of his who is
a medical doctor. "What do you think, Cory? Should I
let them take Carol's knee?"

"Oh, Bob," she replied. "I know that if you could
get Carol to California, there is a doctor who can save
her knee. I think that you must do everything you can to
save it."

After many more phone calls, we learned that in
eighteen hours an air ambulance would arrive to fly
Carol and the rest of us home. We were all ecstatic. This,
we knew would be a major breakthrough.

We said good-bye to a reluctant Jeanne. She
obviously didn't want to go to Jerusalem now for a
whole month, but Mom assured her that she should go
and learn all she could.

As Jim, Gretchen, Mom, Dad, Carol, and I boarded
the tiny Learjet ambulance, we were aware of the many
blessings God had given us. He had spared Carol's life,
He had brought Mom and Dad safely to Iowa in time to
consult the doctor and decide to postpone the surgery
that could have taken Carol's knee, and now He had
provided an air ambulance to take Carol to the best care

possible.

As the tiny jet, cramped for so many people, started its powerful motors and we taxied into position for our takeoff, Dad said, "God has been so good. Let's all thank Him through song."

And as the jet sped through the night, high above the world, one could hear over the roar of the engines a brave family proclaiming:

> Praise God from whom all blessings flow.
> Praise Him, all creatures here below.
> Praise Him above, ye Heavenly Hosts.
> Praise Father, Son, and Holy Ghost!

14

Only the Beginning

"Let's try one more store before we go," I pleaded with my exhausted mother.

"Okay, but I'm afraid that after this one, we'll have to quit for the day. I'm just plain worn out."

Poor Mom. After spending hours by Carol's side at Children's Hospital, she had promised she would go shopping with me for bridesmaids' dresses.

It was no easy task finding a dress sophisticated enough for Jeanne, the college coed, yet sweet enough for twelve-year-old Gretchen. We had looked high and low, and this last store was my final hope.

"Oh, it's perfect!" Mom exclaimed when she saw the dark maroon, taffeta dress. We both fell in love with it immediately.

"It'll look good on everybody, don't you think?"

I asked.

"I think so. I'm sure Jeannie will like it; Gretchen will look pretty as a picture in it; and the style should be easy for Carol to maneuver in."

This was a major consideration. Carol had declared that her first goal was to be able to walk down the aisle at my wedding. Although we had thought that six months would be enough time for her to reach her goal, it was nearly Thanksgiving, the wedding was only three months away, and Carol hadn't even been out of her hospital bed yet.

So many complications had set in: a knee that refused to respond to therapy and germs that had lain dormant then suddenly flared in an infection that raged through her body, bringing with it fever and delirium.

Intravenous feedings and transfusions became increasingly difficult as vein after vein collapsed. One night, as I sat with Carol, a vein collapsed in the middle of a blood transfusion. Its walls had become so stretched that they burst, releasing the incoming blood into the surrounding tissue. The result—an arm that swelled up like a red balloon.

Day after day, week after week, month after month of this went by. Consequently, the majority of my free time was spent at the hospital, and Mom and Dad spent almost every waking hour there. The days ticked off, bringing my wedding alarmingly close.

I think every girl dreams of the time when she and

her mother will plan her wedding. I had waited a long
time to share these precious times with Mom, but now
that they were finally here, they were overshadowed by
Carol's problems. It was difficult for Mom to give me
her full attention when she knew that Carol was in severe
pain, and when she knew that as long as infection flared
uncontrollably, Carol's knee was in danger of being
amputated.

Both Mom and I felt sorry for ourselves at times as
we watched the days fly by and the once-in-a-lifetime
moments slip past, never to be recaptured. Now, we had
finally been able to spend an afternoon together, and we
had successfully found the bridesmaids' dresses.

As I looked at the pretty dress with its unusual plaid
trim, I suddenly thought, "Carol would love to see it!"

So I badgered the saleslady into letting me take her
one-and-only sample dress with me.

I was so excited when I swept into Carol's room
with the rustling, taffeta gown in my arms.

"Carol! Look what Mom and I found today! Do
you like it? The color's perfect for you!"

But Carol's smile was pained. She murmured, "It's
very pretty, Sheila."

With a gulp, I reluctantly put the dress down. Once
more I had to put my own desires aside to give Carol's
immediate needs my full attention.

"What is it, Carol?" I asked. "Is something wrong?"

"Well, I've had a lot of 'phantom pains' today. My
leg hurts just as badly as if it were there."

The doctor had warned us that these would occur.

She could expect them for up to a year, and maybe her whole life. Those severed nerves had to learn to adjust and stop sending pain messages to areas that no longer existed.

"Is that all that's wrong, Carol?"

"No, I guess I've been thinking a lot today about how long it's been since I've been home, and how long it's been since I've walked. Why, Sheila, do you realize that I haven't even been out of this bed for over four months?"

She looked up at me with her gorgeous, clear, blue eyes that look deep and demand the truth. "Sheila," she asked, "Do you think I'll ever be able to walk again?"

"Oh, Carol! Of course you'll be able to walk! And much sooner than you think! Why, when you walk down the aisle at my wedding in this beautiful gown, you'll be the prettiest, most graceful girl there. Besides me, of course!"

Carol's eyes laughed, in spite of her tears. "Nobody's allowed to be prettier than the bride. And I'll bet you'll be the prettiest bride ever!"

Although it wasn't easy planning the wedding at this time in my family's life, it did provide a breath of fresh air for us all. As an event, it signified new beginnings for both Carol and me. It gave Carol a goal. It gave her light at the end of a tunnel of hospital days; and when she would walk down that aisle, she would be on her way back to a normal life.

Because Mom was unable to be as involved in the wedding plans as she would like to have been, Jim filled in gladly. Being an artist, he had definite ideas on every detail, even down to the flower arrangements and the cake decoration. One detail that was carefully kept from him was my dress.

When it came time for my fitting in Los Angeles, Dad decided that he would accompany me. The ride there and back provided a rare opportunity for father and daughter to exchange dreams, goals, hopes.

Dad's dream was to have Carol home—strong and healthy. His goal was to see the Crystal Cathedral, the new church that he was building, dedicated debt-free, without any loans or mortgages attached, so that all the offerings collected within it could be given to mission projects throughout the world. In addition, the standing structure, the Crystal Cathedral, would be an instrument for God where millions of people through the decades would hear the love of Jesus Christ.

After Dad had shared with me, he turned and said, "Sheila, in a few months your dreams will be coming true!"

"Oh, yes, Dad! God has given me a fantastic man!"

"He treats you like a precious teacup, doesn't he."

"He really does! I feel *so* lucky!"

Dad quickly corrected me, "Blessed. Luck has nothing to do with it. God has blessed you with a wonderful man. And He has blessed Jim with a beautiful bride."

"Oh, Dad, just wait until you see my dress! I'm so

grateful to you for buying it for me."

"Well, Sheila, it's my pleasure," he said. "There's no dress in the whole world that I would rather buy for you than your wedding dress. Every bride should have a beautiful dress.

"Some people have said that it's a waste to spend so much money on a dress that's only worn once. Actually, Sheila, you will wear your wedding dress more than any other in your life. You wore it the day you received your first bride doll. And you have worn it every time you have dreamed of your wedding. You will wear it next on your wedding day; and every time you look at your wedding pictures, you will wear it. So you see, that of all the dresses I have ever given you, you will wear this one the most."

It was with eagerness that I slipped into the satin and lace folds as soon as we got to the store. The saleslady carefully arranged the delicate lace veil. I looked at myself in the mirror and quickly tried to clear the tears from my eyes as the image grew hazy. "It's really me!" I thought. "Me—a bride!" My dreams really *were* coming true.

As I emerged from the dressing room and saw Dad with tears in his eyes, and a smile a mile wide, I suddenly realized that I was no longer his little girl. He would no longer be the man in my life.

I had prayed and prayed for a man like Jim, a man who would treat me wonderfully, who would love me deeply, and who would be the source of my dreams and my tomorrows. Now, my prayers had been answered. I

Do I look happy? Am I in love? Is my man handsome? Yes, yes, yes!

felt a deep, deep joy.

Dad took me in his arms and whispered, "You look beautiful! Jim will be so proud of you when he sees you walking down the aisle as his bride!"

"Oh, Dad, do you really think so?"

"Oh, yes! And, Sheila, I am thrilled and delighted to give you to Jim. He's a fine Christian man."

My wedding day was the most glorious of my life. The sun was shining in all its splendor, and it glistened on the many white orchids that graced the sanctuary with a garden freshness. I never felt more beautiful, more loved, or more in love with my groom and my Lord.

Dad and I waited at the back of the sanctuary. He was to walk me down the aisle, give me away, and then perform the ceremony. Everything looked pure and dreamy through my veil. Dad looked as handsome as ever in his robe.

Carol was perched on her crutches, waiting for her cue to start down the aisle. Gretchen, too, was waiting for her entrance. Both were lovely, with touches of flowers at their necks and in their hair.

Jeannie, my maid of honor, turned to me with brimming eyes and said, "Oh, Sheila! The song Barb and Toby are singing is really beautiful!"

It *was* beautiful, and it expressed my feelings so well. I, too, found my eyes filling. And as I saw my handsome groom lead his men across the grass courtyard, I began to bounce excitedly in my

Left to right: Linda (Bob's beautiful wife), Bob, Angie Rae (their darling daughter), Carol, Dad, Me, Jim, Mom, Jeannie, and Gretchen.

white satin ballet slippers. Behind my Jim, loomed the
Good Shepherd statue, my Lord, my Shepherd, my
Jesus, beautifully reinforcing the words of the song:

> Sometimes, not often enough,
> We reflect upon the good things;
> And those thoughts always
> Center around those we love;
> And I think about those people
> Who mean so much to me
> And for so many years have made me
> So very happy;
> And I count the times I have forgotten
> To say, thank you,
> And just how much I love them.

And, oh, how I *do* love them.

Beautiful Carol, who has reached so many of her
goals since the accident—who has been an inspiration to
so many.

Sweet Gretchen—the baby of the family—she's
brought much joy to my life.

Unpredictable, impulsive Jeannie—the fire of the
family. Her dark, brown eyes flash with excitement and
adventure one minute and a deep tenderness the next.

Tall, handsome Bob, no longer the naughty
preacher's son, still an incurable tease but, also, one of
the most gentle and sensitive men I have known.

Mother—my model of what an ideal woman should
be—loving, thoughtful, concerned, caring, soft, and
feminine, and all the while, creatively pursuing her
projects.

And, finally, dear Dad—so dynamic, such a dreamer, a man of high hopes and tremendous accomplishments. But also a man who is first and foremost a family man—a husband and a father—my father, and my friend.

A kiss for Robert Schuller, my father and my friend!